Quentin Blake
Words and Pictures

First published in 2000
3 5 7 9 10 8 6 4
© 2000 Quentin Blake

Quentin Blake has asserted his right under the
Copyright, Designs and Patents Act, 1988,
to be identified as the author and illustrator of this work.

First published in the United Kingdom in 2000 by
Jonathan Cape Ltd
The Random House Group Limited
61-63 Uxbridge Road, London W5 5SA

Random House Australia (Pty) Limited
20 Alfred Street, Milsons Point, Sydney
New South Wales 2061, Australia

Random House New Zealand Limited
18 Poland Road, Glenfield
Auckland 10, New Zealand

Random House South Africa (Pty) Limited
Endulini, 5A Jubilee Road, Parktown 2193, South Africa

The Random House Group Limited Reg. No. 954009
www.**kids**at**randomhouse**.co.uk

A CIP catalogue record for this book is available from the British Library

ISBN 0224032666
Printed and bound in Singapore
by Tien Wah Press

To
The Royal College of Art

Of many friends in publishing I would in particular like to thank Christine Baker who, with Pierre Marchand, the former director of Gallimard Jeunesse, has published so many of my books in France and who was responsible for *La Vie de la Page* in which many of the observations in this book first found expression.

I am also grateful to Chris Beetles for his energy and experience. His gallery in Ryder Street has seen three exhibitions of my work, including the most recent one which celebrates the publication of this book.

Thanks are also due to Hilary Rubinstein and Caradoc King, past and present directors of A.P. Watt, for their constant care of my interests; and to my wonderful support team of Sally Carr (who for many years now has made my working life better) Nikki Mansergh and Vicki Bingham. Like their predecessors, they deal courageously with the problems created by someone who does far too many drawings.

In dedicating this book to the Royal College of Art I want to express my gratitude to that great institution. Teaching there has been a constant stimulus to me, and the college has been the source of close and lasting friendships: Linda Kitson, Dan Fern, Alison Britton, Emma Chichester Clark, and so many more. Amongst them I salute too the memory of Brian Robb, teacher, painter and illustrator. His words were wise and his pictures were distinctively his own; my life, like that of many other artists, was enriched by knowing him.

Lady and Frog, 1976

The Simple Life

As its title explains, this is a book of words and pictures. The pictures are a selection of my work from over the past fifty years. Many of them are from books which are still in print, and some are quite well known; but I hope you may also be interested to look at others which you may not have seen before, either because they are preliminary working drawings which have never before been published, or because they come from books and magazines long out of print.

It's quite possible simply to look at the pictures and not read the words at all; but if you do you will find that this is not for the most part a book about reminiscence – it is not about my life apart from work, or about the twenty years I spent teaching illustration at the Royal College of Art. However, it does bring together a number of thoughts that I have expressed in talks and conversations at one time or another; and I hope that, in explaining how I set about my own work, I may say some things which are of interest to other illustrators – particularly those just starting out – as well as to the readers of the books I have illustrated, whether they are teachers, parents or children.

Where I have not altogether followed my own principle of not including reminiscence is in the early pages of the book; and that is because I think that experience of getting started – how you find out who you are as an artist, how you get yourself into some situation where people will want to buy your work, and so on – can be of help and interest.

I can remember myself, for instance, aged sixteen, sitting in the waiting-room of the (then very famous) humorous magazine *Punch*. In those days the *Punch* office was a rather imposing building off Fleet Street, full of heavy furniture and men in important-looking suits, as though it were a cross between a private club and the Ministry of Humorous Observation. I was there because a couple of years previously I had made the acquaintance of a painter and cartoonist called Alfred Jackson, the husband of a teacher at my school; and subsequently, with his advice and encouragement, I had been submitting drawings to *Punch*; all rejected, albeit with notes of "not quite this time …" which seemed to mean "try again". I had

One of the first drawings accepted by Punch *in 1949.*

Opposite and following page, original artwork for full-page drawings in Punch.

"LOOK, MISS JENKINS, WE'VE GOT THIS ONE TWICE!"

decided that it might be a good idea to go and see the art editor in person, and his willingness to see me had taken me to the *Punch* office. A secretary had put me in the waiting room next to a woman artist who was also waiting and given me magazines to look at. I discovered later she was an illustrator of the time whom I very much admired, Pearl Falconer, and I wished later that I had spoken to her. At any rate, in due course she disappeared and I went on reading magazines. Time passed.

Early Punch *drawing.*

Eventually the secretary returned and was amazed to find me still there: it had been assumed that this teenage schoolboy with the hair flopping over his forehead belonged to the other visitor. Alas, it was now too late for the art editor to see me. However, on my next visit I did see him, and he accepted two very small drawings and started me off drawing for *Punch* for the next forty years. In those days a small drawing was paid for by a cheque for seven guineas. I didn't have a bank account so that when I got the first cheque I didn't know what to do with it.

I was, needless to say, very excited to see even a small drawing in print; what I wasn't aware of at that time was that I was setting out on a familiar route, because many cartoonists and humorous illustrators have worked on books for children. Dicky Doyle, for instance, had started when he was a teenager. The difference

Drawing submitted for 'A' Level Art.

between us was that I just managed to scrape over the line, whereas, at sixteen, he was already an extraordinarily gifted draughtsman who could draw anything. Later on, when he fell out with *Punch*, he did some very good drawings for *The King of the Golden River* by John Ruskin and for a series of Fairy Books. George Cruikshank, having started young as an apprentice to his father, the cartoonist Isaac Cruikshank, became the illustrator of *Oliver Twist* as well as *Grimms' Fairy Tales* and many other books. Other nineteenth century figures such as Tenniel and Caldecott, though less early starters, began as journalists and later included book illustration in their repertoire.

At the time I wasn't thinking about any of this. Nor, I think, was I aware that what I was starting on was also for me a sort of apprenticeship. What I mean by that is that I didn't learn how to draw and then find a way of using that skill but, like an assistant in a blacksmith's shop or in a fifteenth century artist's studio, I started straightaway at simple tasks and learned the job as I was doing it by looking at the work of experienced craftsmen. (This is rather different from the art school tradition, where in broad terms you learn how to draw and then apply the skill later.)

Scraperboard drawings for the school magazine, 'The Chronicle'.

Another moment that, looking back, I can see was of importance was a school visit of a group of us, at about the same time as my visit to the Punch office, to the first showing in London of the Marcel Carné film *Les Enfants du Paradis*. One of my companions wrote an account of the visit for the school magazine. I can still remember the final words of it: "We came away thinking about Arletty." Well, she was an extraordinary actress, and we certainly did. But I also took away with me the effect of another sequence of images. It was of Jean-Louis Barrault as the son of the Debureau family, and in particular of that scene when he is sitting on a barrel outside the Théâtre des Funambules in clown's costume, with his arms and legs hanging down as though he were a puppet, until the moment when he is able to come to life, as it were, and act the story of the little pick-pocketing incident which has taken place in front of him. That moment, with all its accompanying atmosphere, is something that has stayed with me. It represents for me that mime element which is an important part of illustration as I understand it – of telling the story by acting it.

*Two pages of drawings submitted for
'A' Level Art.*

Another visual influence – this time an artist – was the nineteenth century French artist, Honoré Daumier. I can remember buying, on another trip to London, a book of reproductions of his lithographs. It was the most expensive book I had ever bought (two guineas – two pounds and two shillings!) and I can remember my mother saying, "Do you really want to spend all this money on a book?" I remember too how taken I was with the look of it – a large flat book with a pink cover almost like a portfolio, and its generous elegant title page. But it was the contents that were important. Daumier did over four thousand lithographs in his lifetime for the humorous Parisian newspapers *Charivari* and *La Caricature* and satire was their *raison d'être* ; but, as Baudelaire pointed out, he had Michelangelo "under his skin". There was nothing slight about his pictures, and he knew everything about showing a situation visually – his characters live out their lives against the shadow of the Parisian streets with an extraordinary intensity.

I will come back to the question of influences; but while assembling this brief list of remembered early moments I can perhaps add one more snapshot. At the age of nineteen I was called up to do two years' military service and spent my time in the Royal Army Educational Corps teaching reading and writing to boy-soldiers in Aldershot. I had published a few drawings in the Army magazine, *Soldier*, as well as my drawings in *Punch* and when these were noticed I was sent to spend three weeks at the headquarters of the RAEC re-illustrating a booklet – *English Parade* – used in teaching those soldiers who hadn't yet mastered reading. I was given to understand that the colonel who revised the text was paid an honorarium; there was no alteration to my weekly pay-packet, but I was excused boots. Although only forty pages, *English Parade* can claim, I suppose, to be the first book that I illustrated; it is also the only book that I have illustrated wearing uniform. In that respect it was truly a stage in my apprenticeship: not only did I have to produce a continuous series of related drawings but also, from time to time, I had to take them to show to a lieutenant-colonel for his comment and

Illustration for English Parade.

approval. A few moments of silence as he sat behind his desk and I stood, at ease, in front of it. Then:

"Very good, Sergeant Blake. But I think … the grass in this one ought to be shorter."

"Yes sir. I'll see to it, sir."

"And I think the creases in these trousers might be a little bit sharper."

The problem with making grass shorter in drawings is that you can't cut it: you have to do the drawing again. But if there was no chance of artistic rebellion here, there was at least a preparation for encounters with editors and (worse) committees, later on.

Illustration for English Parade, *with short grass.*

The drawings that I did for *English Parade* were done in the same way that I did my drawings for *Punch* at that time. It was a simple technique. In those days if you read a book about drawing for the press it probably told you that you had to draw in intensely black ink on brilliant white paper to ensure faithful reproduction. A little later I was delighted to see some originals of drawings by Ronald Searle, which I very much admired and which were drawn with a fountain-pen filled with some kind of dark purplish furniture-stain. To see them was for me a step in the direction of enlightenment, but I couldn't manage to do my early drawings like that. I drew them in soft pencil first, and then inked in the outlines, being careful not to let fall a blot of ink that might ruin the drawing. Then, when the ink was thoroughly dry, I rubbed out the pencil lines. Eventually, however, two things helped me to change my method of drawing and find the way that I use now. One was that after a while I began to submit to *Punch* not finished drawings, but roughs; and now and then it became apparent that there were things in these roughs – moments of fluency, atmosphere, expression – that I wasn't capturing in the finished drawing. (Probably every illustrator is familiar with this experience.) And once or twice the art editor, Russell Brockbank, though a man of very controlled and organised drawing himself, actually printed the rough in preference to the finished drawing.

'Children's library'. A set of drawings from Punch.

Headings for Punch's *weekly page of financial and country notes.*

Full page illustration for Granta.

The other discovery was that there wasn't, after all, such a need to be anxious about mistakes (at least with black and white printing – I hadn't yet found my way into colour) and if I made a blot I could get some process white and paint it out. And not only that; I discovered that if necessary you could do an extra bit of drawing and stick it on and when it was printed it didn't show. For a while my drawings developed into a sort of collage of cut-out pieces of paper while I tried to get the very best result. (Once or twice I even found myself with a dot for an eye on a tiny scrap of paper, moving it around with a pin to get the best expression.) But this wasn't the main advantage, which was that now I could feel relaxed about producing a drawing and, curiously enough, if you are more relaxed you can concentrate better, you are able to focus your mind on exactly what is happening in front of you, the scene that you are imagining in your mind and living through the pen you are holding in your hand. I began to enjoy the scratchiness and fluency of the nib as it instinctively searched out what I was trying to draw. My drawing became what my friend the French illustrator Philippe Dumas described as *"une écriture"* – a sort of handwriting.

It was on account of this relaxation – or increased concentration – that I really began to learn about drawing and what I could do with it. There were also other encouraging influences; for instance, the work of the French illustrator, André François. At that time, in the fifties, his work was to be seen in English magazines like *Punch* and *Lilliput* as well as on extraordinarily imaginative posters in Paris and London. The importance for me was that he was not at all frightened of the business of illustration and he brought to it not only amazing ingenuity but all the techniques of the arts of painting and drawing; anything you can do in painting he was ready to do in illustration. A drawing could not only fulfil its commercial function, but do it with panache: still be scratchy and instinctive and badly-behaved.

Of course François was not my only influence. If you illustrate books and, in particular, if you illustrate children's books, people seem to like to ask you who has influenced you, and sometimes you can tell that they expect you to say the name of one other children's book illustrator. Mostly, however, artists do illustration because they want to do some kind of art, and if they have any ambition for their work they will want to pay homage to the

very best: so that I could mention Rembrandt, Picasso, Goya, Rowlandson, George Cruikshank and dozens of other names. Every artist will have his or her own list.

Once I had stopped being a student I was no longer restricted to submitting cartoons to magazines; on the basis of my printed work I could go and look for other work which might extend my range and offer me new problems to think about. At Cambridge I had not done a great deal of drawing but I had contributed to one or two issues of the undergraduate magazine *Granta*. One of the people who had been involved with *Granta*, Rory McEwen, had gone on to work for the political and literary magazine *The Spectator* and was able to invite me to do some drawings for it. In due course I took on the job of doing most of the covers; it offered an enormous variety of subjects to be treated, but the theme of each cover was normally only decided a day or two – sometimes as little as hours – before the finished drawing was needed, so that what was to be drawn and how it was to be drawn had to be decided quickly. It meant that things often went wrong; but also that it was possible to try experiments. All this was wonderful for the apprenticeship, and I suppose, with the requirement to play a different part every week, corresponded to the experience that an actor gains in playing repertory. At the same time I began to find other tasks: some advertising; covers for Penguin Books such as the novels of Evelyn Waugh and Malcolm Bradbury; and the books of the humorous writer Patrick Campbell, whom I had first illustrated in the pages of *The Spectator*.

SPECTATOR

Christmas Number

2/-

Hesketh Pearson

John Betjeman

Evelyn Waugh

Patrick Campbell

Angus Wilson

Bernard Levin

Cyril Ray

Roy Jenkins

Kingsley Amis

NUMBER 6856   FRIDAY, NOVEMBER 20, 1959

Spectator

number 7150   Friday July 9 1965   one shilling

William
Warbey, MP
Failure of
A Mission

Revolt at
No. 10

The Monster
at Heathrow

Another
'Non!'

Spectator

SUMMER
BOOKS

John Betjeman
A. Alvarez
Sir Denis Brogan
Marcus Cunliffe
William Plomer
John Terraine
Hugh Seton-Watson
John Erickson
Peter Vansittart
Michael Hamburger
John Davenport

Quentin Blake

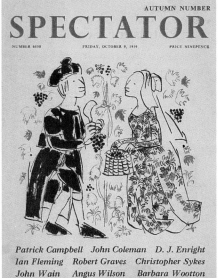

CHRISTMAS NUMBER. 2/-

*Headings in cut paper
for the Arts pages of
The Spectator.*

Above, an illustration for Rough Husbandry.
Right, the cover and an illustration from Come
Here Till I Tell You.

*Facing page, original artwork for a Christmas
number of* The Spectator.

Life drawing from Chelsea School of Art.

Painting in oil on hardboard from the fifties.

Extending my range made me all the more conscious of my lack of experience of life drawing – I just didn't have enough knowledge to draw the things I needed to draw. While I was looking for a life-class that I might join I came across an article in an art magazine about the artist Brian Robb. I knew his work already from his illustrations to Sterne's *Tristram Shandy*; and now I learned that he was both illustrator and painter; had formerly drawn in *Punch* and the magazine *Night and Day*; was teaching at the Chelsea School of Art. He sounded like the sort of person who could give me the advice I needed; and so he was. It's strange how sometimes one has the instinct to do the right thing; something that will go on having an effect throughout your life.

One of the effects of finding and getting to know Brian Robb was that, several years later, he invited me to go and work for him at the Royal College of Art, where I eventually took over from him as head of the Illustration Department. But in the first instance he advised me not to join his illustration group; he talked to me about my drawings; and he introduced me to one of the Chelsea life-classes. I attended one or two days a week for about eighteen months. At that time, life-drawing in most schools had either been phased out altogether in favour of Basic Design; or was only taught in a formal way that didn't give any thought to its eventual use and effect. Many students attended because it was a duty; by contrast I was there to get some useful element in my diet that had hitherto been lacking.

Most of the drawings I did were neither good drawings nor attractive-looking ones. It's important, I'm sure, to regard life-drawings as work drawings and not to think too much about the final appearance. But sometimes I would turn away from the model and draw what I could remember (interesting to notice how different that is from what you see in front of you); and at the end of the day I would go home and invent some more life-drawings from memory. In front of the model and away from the model I was trying to establish some kind of balance between seeing and imagining; so much of the essence of drawing is in imagining what you are drawing, of trying to feel the balance, the gesture; of trying to become the subject.

In the same way I also did life-paintings; and these life-room experiences, life-room memories, developed first into drawings done with a plastic quill, and partly coloured, and not much later into paintings of the nude done with house-painting brushes and colours that were more emotional than naturalistic. Someone described them at the time as "subaqueous"; when I returned to paint more of them in later years the colours got less murky but the subaqueous feel was still there and some of them actually became swimmers. In some ways what they seem to be is the opposite of my illustration – they're introspective, not very active; the strokes are broad, not precise; and so on. This "fine art" activity has gone on, intermittently, like some kind of buried stream; and though it surfaces from time to time, I've never gone back seriously to the life-class, despite sometimes resolving to do so. My most recent work of this kind is a set of large watercolour drawings, twenty of which make up a portfolio-size volume entitled *Woman with a Book*. Although in some ways they are not unlike life-class drawings, they are actually done without models and improvised on the page.

Facing page, drawings from memory done at home with a plastic quill.

'Floorscape' and 'Wave', two paintings from the eighties. The one above is four feet square.

Following page, from Woman with a Book, *1999.*

To return to the urge to draw which is the basic drive of the illustrator; the instinct to seek out exciting, rewarding subjects that will satisfy that appetite. Perhaps he or she is not so very different from a child badgering its parents: "What shall I draw now? What shall I draw now?" Fortunately you are not applying to your parents, and the answer comes either from your own imagination or from the imaginations of authors; sometimes the answers they give can be quite unexpected. For instance, many years ago, without any thought of illustration, I bought a paper-

back from one of those second-hand book stalls along the quais of the Seine in Paris. I still have it, falling to pieces now, that copy of Cyrano de Bergerac's *Voyages to the Moon and to the Sun*. I don't really know any more why I bought it – perhaps it was the engraving on the cover which attracted me – but I read it and was fascinated by it. I started to illustrate it for its own sake without being commissioned by any publisher, and eventually I suggested it as an idea to The Folio Society. It is to some extent like *Gulliver's Travels*, although written perhaps a hundred years before that book: similar in that it describes the world of the Moon and the world of the Sun and what the people are like there and how they live, as Swift does with Lilliput and Brobdingnag. But of course they are not really those places – they are imaginary worlds which the writer invents to parody the world as we know it. Cyrano's book is full of interest in intellectual and

Cyrano and the Royal Trainer

scientific ideas, in the manners and customs of the time, and explores them in a lively and provocative sort of way. More than that, it contains just so many things to draw.

In these invented worlds there are people much larger than we are; so there are differences of scale. They wear no clothes; so there are opportunities for life-drawing. There are aristocrats who communicate by playing the lute and working people who communicate by gesticulation. Indeed, the possibilities of all kinds of activity are manifold. What could be nicer than the moment when the royal monkey-trainer thinks that Cyrano is another curious variant of the breed and begins to teach him tricks? Or the musket which brings down birds not just dead but stuffed and ready for the oven? Or the unfortunate Cyrano, found guilty by the birds of the crime of being human, carried to the place of the Sad Death on the back of a black ostrich?

When I took my first steps in book illustration I found that I had entered a sort of enchanted grove where there were things to draw at every turn. Since I had no idea how you arranged to get to illustrate a children's book I asked my friend John Yeoman to write one for me, and *A Drink of Water* provided me straightaway with both humans and animals – assorted birds, a warthog, a monkey, a bear. There were more humans and animals in *Listen and I'll Tell You* by Edward Korel and *My Son-in-Law the Hippopotamus* by 'Ezo' and then, amongst the first of my books for Jonathan Cape, *Uncle* revealed a rich seam of possibilities. *Uncle* was the first of a series of six books, a gathering together of the stories that J.P. Martin, a former Methodist minister, had invented for his children.

They concerned a rich patriarchal elephant, normally wearing a purple dressing-gown, and his hangers-on; and opposed to them, the Badfort crowd, a hairy crew given to jeering and bad behaviour. J.P. Martin's strong suit was not so much the development of plot as the ability to produce bizarre new characters with extraordinary names (Hitmouse, Jellytussle, Waldovenison Smeare) seemingly with every chapter. I was never at a loss for subject-matter, and the only problem, as I remember it, was that the bristly dirty people were so enjoyable that I tended to produce a disproportionately large number of pictures for them.

Four pages from A Drink of Water.

From My Son-in-Law the Hippopotamus

From Listen and I'll Tell You.

From Uncle *and* Uncle Cleans Up.

Drawings from the first version of
The Boy Who Sprouted Antlers *of 1961.*

The second version of 1976, redrawn because small boys had started wearing long trousers.

The towers and waterfalls and swamps of *Uncle* were important, but the scenery was not as important to me as the characters in front of it. That is nearly always so, and if I track forward to a book of my own such as *All Join In* it is evident, I think, that it is less a collection of verses to be illustrated than a collection of activities looking for words. There is plenty of running about and jumping up and down; and not to hold up these activities, I draw in only as much background as is necessary. I do, however, provide the necessary furniture and accessories: the musical instruments when the children all play together; the sofa from which the sleeping Oscar leaps; the objects used in the mouse-chase; and the inadequate chair rushed on to support the fainting Grandma. (This is not a piece of anti-grandmotherism, incidentally. We know that grandmothers nowadays are dynamic and full of energy; but it's also true that to small children many adults are large and strange and inconvenient; and that is one of the things that this drawing is about.)

Now and then I have been asked why I think children like my drawings: a question which maybe should be addressed to the people who look at my pictures, not to me. But I have come to suspect that one of the reasons may be that these drawings are like something happening. There is some sequence of time implied in them; an arm may be as much the description of a gesture as a depiction of anatomy. It's a sort of little theatre. Look, for instance, at the daily life of Simpkin: no scenery, just stage props when they are needed. Simpkin acts his life: he is such a nuisance simply because, like most children, he is in the ecstasy of being.

Simpkin
ROUND and ROUND
the chairs

Simpkin UP

and DOWN the stairs

And when Granny's going to faint
We ALL JOIN IN

But the very best of all is when
we ALL JOIN IN

When Oscar's on the sofa
  and he's curled up fast asleep
We know he likes a serenade —

We go BEEP-BEEP BEEP-BEEP

There are one or two things learned as a cartoonist that can help the artist in setting about a book. The first is that it is not necessarily part of the job to copy nature, or to convey anything but a selection of visual information. What you have to do essentially is to use a set of signals; to convey to the spectator economically what is happening in the picture; how the participants are reacting, in a simplified, almost diagrammatic form. Of course, it still has to be one that has its own kind of life. Second, there must be some sense of timing, of choosing the right moment. I do a freewheeling sort of drawing that looks as though it is done on the spur of the moment but the problem is that for a book, as distinct from a single drawing, a certain amount of planning is essential: What goes on which page? Do the actions carry on from one picture to another? Do the characters still look the same on each page? In the attempt to combine planning with an air of spontaneity I've employed various techniques of which the one I have found most successful, and have used for the last twenty years, makes use of a light box. On the light box I put the rough drawing I am going to work from, and on top of that a sheet of watercolour paper,

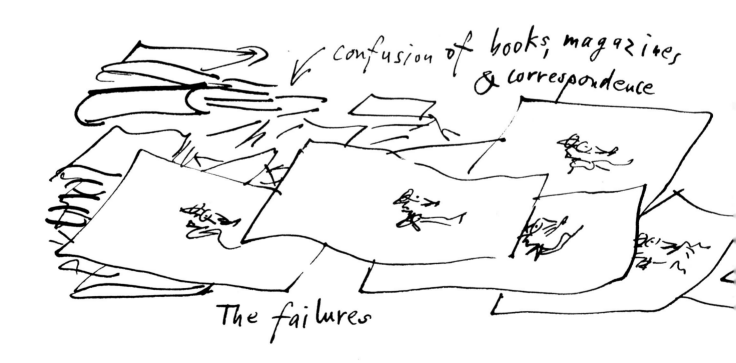

confusion of books, magazines & correspondence

The failures

normally Canson or Arches fin. Ready to hand is a bottle of waterproof black ink and a lot of scruffy-looking dip pens. Essentially each of these is a straight double-ended holder (a German make called Brause) with a nib, most usually a Waverley (originally intended as a writing nib), which is flexible and scratchy, or a J nib, which is harder and broader. Or it may be some other kind of nib, or a brush, or a reed pen, depending on the needs of the job. What happens next is not tracing; in fact it's important that I can't see the rough drawing underneath too clearly, because when I draw I try to draw as if for the first time; but I can do it with increased concentration, because the drawing underneath lets me know all the elements that have to appear and exactly where they have to be placed. Normally I begin with the most difficult piece of the drawing – some particular facial expression, some particular gesture or stance – so that if I get that wrong, I don't have to repeat the whole of the drawing. Consequently, it's not impossible for me to find myself at the end of a session of work surrounded by expensive sheets of watercolour paper with a small face bearing not quite the right expression in the middle of each.

Aa

A is for Apples,
some green and some red

Work on a book (one for which I haven't written my own words, that is) begins when the typescript arrives from the publisher; and it begins with reading. In a sense I'm reading the story as if I were two people at the same time: a normal reader, who is relishing a good story for its own sake; and an illustrator, who is on the look-out for good subjects to draw, good moments. I probably read the story several times to get to know it, and I make underlinings and notes in the margin so that I can easily find the bits I want to refer back to later.

Most of my choices I make by what feels like instinct; but when I look back on them I can see that what the illustrations are doing is not always quite the same thing on each occasion. Though *Quentin Blake's ABC* is by me, and not by another writer, the pictures in it enable me to show the relationship between text and pictures in a clear and simple fashion. Standing on its own the text doesn't look like anything much; partly because it was adapted to the understanding of small readers but even more because it was written with an eye to the ways it could trigger off drawings.

O is for Ostrich
who gives us a ride

A is for Apples,
some green and some red

is straightforward enough, and there are the apples. The idea of this book, however, was not to show still life, but activity; so there are not only apples in the required colours, but there is also this well-dressed gent juggling with them, and the children looking on. The illustration has expanded the possibilities of the text; we are already into an unexpected situation. It's noticeable that

O is for Ostrich
who gives us a ride

is (along with the Yak that appears later) the most exotic item in the text, so that it's sufficient to supply a quite straightforward depiction: there it is.

P is for Parcel –
let's guess what's inside

by contrast, makes an invitation to speculate, helped by the picture. What is inside? A collection of objects? A tractor's exhaust pipe? An oven-ready ostrich? The illustrator of children's books has to think not only of the appearance of the drawing itself but also how the drawing is going to be "used" by the

P is for Parcel –
let's guess what's inside

G is for Grandma –
she's really quite fat

M is for Mud
that we get on our knees

reader; how it's going to figure in the social situation of reading. If we go back once again in the alphabet we can see that

L is for Legs
that we wave in the air

is just mischievous, and is entirely for the sake of the picture, while

G is for Grandma –
she's really quite fat

offers a gentle exploration of the possibilities: the cakes that may have made their contribution; her cat that seems to have been on a similar diet; and can that picture on the wall be one of her in younger days?

M is for Mud
that we get on our knees

could, if you kept close to the text, remain a fairly tame idea. What is attractive is that, in the exploration of mud, it's possible to set up a little tension between word and picture. We can see that it isn't only on our knees that we get the mud; the picture is beginning to develop into a sequence, a story; and with the little girl with the parasol we are offered the opportunity to look forward to the moment when she hits the mud, and to speculate on subsequent developments.

Since illustrations may be fulfilling a variety of tasks, this choice of moments in the manuscript is important. Where the words of a picture book are concerned, you will find that the shrewd writer has not infrequently incorporated moments which ask to be illustrated. I have worked with John Yeoman for as long as I have illustrated children's books, so I have had plenty of time to learn that he is someone who has a good eye for this; in fact he has said to me: "I see them in pictures." If you look at the pictures from *Up With Birds!* later in this book you will find a wonderful moment which he has invented when the birds who haven't yet found out how to fly take off with their balloons. It's something that comes alive for you on the page.

And of course there are sometimes moments which can't be ignored: in *Don Quixote*, for instance, there are celebrated incidents which I think the reader would expect to see in any version. I think of the knight tilting at windmills or Sancho Panza tossed in a blanket. This latter has a particular appeal for me –

Ll

L is for Legs
that we wave in the air

there is something fascinating in being able to preserve that airborne moment: of the same kind there's the little girl with her parasol, Clown being thrown by the skinhead, the boy with the liquorice allsorts in *Matilda*.

Matilda is an example of a book where, for its hundred drawings, there were a lot of choices to be made. Julius Rottwinkle, for instance, the boy with the liquorice allsorts, had been caught by the terrifying Miss Trunchbull eating them under the desk in a scripture lesson and she had thrown him out of the classroom window. It was enjoyable to show him flying through the air, and use the scatter of allsorts to describe his trajectory. It's an incident that doesn't add anything to the advancement of the story, but it benefits from visual treatment, so that you can relish it at leisure; and it makes its contribution to the atmosphere and legend of the story.

There is also the episode of the chocolate cake. Those who have read the story will remember that Bruce Bogtrotter, who had eaten some chocolate cake that wasn't meant for him, was to be punished by having to consume another whole cake in front of the assembled children of the school. To the disgust of Miss Trunchbull, the boy succeeds; in fact, she is so enraged that she picks up the empty plate and smashes it down over the boy's head. (Fortunately he is by now so anaesthetised with cake as to feel nothing.) It seemed to me that the moment for illustration

was the one of anticipation, when the teacher has lifted the plate. If you are a new reader turning the pages of the book, this ought to seize your attention; but it is still left to the author to bring the story to a climax. The writer and the artist are not always trying to do exactly the same thing.

The choice of moments, and a sense of discretion about what to draw and what not to draw, is particularly important in the business of the illustration of poetry, and I was made particularly aware of it when, nearly twenty five years ago, I was invited to do drawings for Michael Rosen's first book of poems, *Mind Your Own Business*. Pam Royds, who was the editor of the book, set about it in what seemed to me then, and still seems to me now, a very open-minded and farsighted way. She brought the three of us together at an early stage when nothing had been established beyond the determination to make an appropriate book out of a mass of Michael Rosen's poems. It's perhaps hard to recall that at that time it was very difficult to sell anything more than a very small edition of a book of poems for children, at least outside an anthology. Characteristically, such a volume would be slim, with a little trickle of words down the centre of the page. There might be some small decorative vignettes, and there was an indefinable air of restrictive virtue.

The poems that Michael Rosen had written made us want to get away from all this; and as I was involved to some extent in the design of the book as well as the illustration, I put forward the idea of a squarish page with plenty of elbow-room. Mostly we didn't give the poems titles and I sited them on the page so that they sat at the bottom rather than hung down from the top. Some pages had only words; others only drawings; the feeling we wanted to give was of a sketchbook or notebook, easy of access. The emphasis of the book is on boys' activities and reactions; Michael Rosen's eye for this, his detailed recollection of boyhood, is incomparable. It was this aspect of the book that I wanted to reflect in the drawings. There were one or two poems that seemed better without illustration – one for instance about a boy in bed listening to his heart beating; to balance these pages which were pure text we had some which were only drawing. For these Michael Rosen gave me some ideas – ideas that he hoped to write verses about one day, but hadn't done so yet. So there is, for instance, a duel in the kitchen which is pure Michael Rosen but drawn instead of written.

Although there is often in Michael Rosen's books a sudden twist or flight of fantasy, they are essentially about everyday life; so that I tried to do drawings that, though they have an element of exaggeration in them, might perhaps have been done on the spot. None of them were done from life, needless to say, but my hope was that by using a sort of fibre-tipped pen which gives a slightly broken line I might be able to create the feeling that they had been drawn into this sketchbook-like volume in a quite impromptu way. (Joanna Carey reports a parent at the time exclaiming: "Just look at the state of these drawings. They aren't even finished properly!")

MRS TOWNSEND

Every time I see Mrs Townsend
she says
O I remember you, you rascal
I can see it now
Your mum and dad was out
looking for you
you was only three
you had gone missing.

You know where they found you?
Halfway up the road
outside the methodist church
running along in your little vest
you didn't have nothing else on
you had left home
with just your vest on
everything else open to the weather
can you imagine?

Well you would never think of that
to look at you now,
would you?

NO

THE ITCH

If your hands get wet
in the washing-up water,
if they get covered in flour,
if you get grease or oil
all over your fingers,
if they land up in the mud,
wet grit, paint, or glue ...

have you noticed
it's just then
that you always get
a terrible itch
just inside your nose?
And you can try to
twitch your nose,
twist your nose,
squeeze your nose,
scratch it with your arm,
scrape your nose on
your shoulder
or press it
up against the wall,
but it's no good.
You can't get rid of
the itch.
It drives you so mad
you just have to let a
finger get at it.
And before you know
you've done it.
you've wiped a load of glue,
or oil,
or cold wet pastry
all over the end of your nose.

Two pages of illustrations from Quick,
Let's Get Out Of Here! *by Michael
Rosen.*

Another aspect of illustration where a measure of sensitivity and discretion is called for is in the depiction of characters. It's sensitive not only because of the possible reactions of the author but also because we all have our own individual visualisations, to a greater or lesser extent, of what we read. (I remember this being underlined for me in conversation with a father who was in the middle of reading *The BFG* to his son. He pointed out that the giant he thought he was reading about was in some way in competition with the one I had drawn. "And," he added, with a touch of parental vexation, "you are winning.")

If you want to be right, but don't feel that you have to win hands down, as an illustrator, there is some help in the nature of illustration itself. It's hand-drawn, it needn't have the documentary insistence of a photograph, and consequently there does seem to be a kind of tolerance that the imagination of the reader can work within; an interplay with both the text and the pictures.

For all that, the illustrator has to make his own effort to visualise a character in his own way, and it is not always an easy business. Dahl's books supply me with the most striking examples, and to describe those I have to explain a little how we worked together. It began, as always, with reading. After that I would produce rough sketches of likely incidents throughout the book and at the same time rather more developed drawings of what I thought the characters looked like; all of which I would in due course take down to Great Missenden where we would sit and go through the drawings, and I would get Dahl's comments.

One difference between the way that a writer works and that of an illustrator is that the writer can put in description when he feels like it. When a character is introduced he can say what he or she is wearing, and doesn't have to refer to it again. (He can even mention, on page 293, that the hero has a moustache of which no mention has been made up to that point. It pays to remain on the alert.)

It was this that provided the problem with the BFG. In the original version of the manuscript the giant was wearing a big leather apron and knee-length boots. They were only mentioned once but naturally they had to appear in every one of my drawings. Roald began to feel that the apron got in the way as

An old shirt
with a pocket with
a hole.

Leather
waistcoat
with pockets

I dont know what these things are called — a sort of leather pocket

leather waistcoat —
shirt with pocket

the giant moved and ran and jumped; that it was more an encumbrance than a help; and that the boots were just visually dull. So round the dining table we sat down to re-think the costume, and I started (as I remember, then and there) to make new sketches to his suggestions. In the end the item that was left unresolved was what the BFG should wear on his feet. Several days later I received through the post a rather oddly-shaped and oddly-wrapped brown paper parcel (parcels seem to have a significant role to play at various points in this book). Unwrapping it revealed a large sandal of a type unfamiliar to me; I soon discovered that it was Norwegian and one of Roald's own. If you want to know what it looked like you can see in the pictures: it is what the BFG wears. Apart from being the happiest solution, the arrival of the sandal, together with other reworking and discussions, brought home to me the closeness of the author to his creation. It didn't, as has on occasion been claimed, lead me to base the BFG on Dahl; the BFG has his own personality and appearance; but there are resemblances and affinities, and being aware of that helped me, I believe, to give him more depth and humanity.

I had another surprise when I drew little Sophie, just as described in the book with her big spectacles, and found out later on that she did exist and that the drawing looked very much like.

When I was at work on the drawings for *Matilda* a similar process took place. The problem was the dreadful headmistress, Miss Trunchbull. In my drawing I had carefully followed the description of this frightening figure; she wore a shirt, collar and tie, belt and boots. Roald had exaggerated; I had exaggerated; what resulted would scarcely have been a flattering portrait of a South American general. It was too much. Roald set us off again in search of a character who was formidable but at least human. He found a photograph of someone he had had in mind when first imagining Miss Trunchbull. The shirt became a garment which was identifiably feminine; the boots became shoes; she developed a stern coiffure; and it became possible to believe that she had once been an Olympic athlete – even if one who was prepared to seize little girls by their pigtails and throw them into the middle distance.

A sort of leather jerkin

The development of Miss Trunchbull.

By comparison it seems to me even now that there would be practically nothing to say about Matilda herself. But looking back at my preliminary drawings I can see that she too developed. The early drawings gave her the childlike face which would really belong to her age; but Matilda is a little girl with an unusual brain and extraordinary capabilities, which I tried to suggest by giving her a face which avoided the characteristic rounded cheeks and forehead and suggested an older child.

She still has to be very small, to emphasise the contrast with the adults. Dahl observed to me in a letter at the time:

'What particularly delights me is the fact that you have accentuated, by all sorts of subtle juxtapositions, the tinyness of Matilda.

Nearly everyone wanted her bigger, but the whole charm of it is that she is so frail and titchy. You have brought that out beautifully, especially when sitting in an armchair or reaching up for something. Great.

The parents are fine,

The librarian is fine,

Miss Honey is lovely.

Now, here are new pages for pages 45 and 46 which re-describe the Trunchbull's looks and her clothes. These descriptions can still be altered if you had any different ideas, but the galleys arrive on November 23rd and very soon after that everything will be set. Page 136 will now contain a small change so that you can fade out with Miss Honey holding Matilda in her arms. The last sentence of all to read (Miss Honey was still hugging the tiny girl in her arms and neither of them ...)'

There is another problem about the depiction of characters. It's one that, on the whole, illustrators don't like to talk about very much – partly because it is difficult and partly because it may not seem to have much to do with art. It is the problem of likeness; of, once you have decided what a character looks like, convincing the reader that it is always the same person. You are lucky if the character has a strong visual clue which helps to establish their identity.

Aunt Fidget Wonkham-Strong, for instance, in *How Tom Beat Captain Najork and His Hired Sportsmen*, has an iron hat, which gives a very clear signal from the start; prompted by that I gave her eyes that gleam through her spectacles, and a trap-like mouth. (There are also other features which don't belong to her face but which help to contribute to her character: a Victorian bustle; a bosom ornamented with sharp pins and brooches; a floor-length dress that suggests that she may have no legs at all but some other form of locomotion.) In addition to this you seem, with repeated drawings, to learn the character; so that after a while you can produce another drawing and know whether it looks like him or her.

However, the illustrator's responsibility doesn't end when he has done his best to assist in the depiction of his author's characters. He also has to attempt to reflect the whole atmosphere of the work and to give the reader some signals about the kind of book it is. There is a very important role for the publisher or editor to play here: to put together the right artist with the right author. If the match is a good one the publisher strangely becomes invisible; the reader won't even think about the publisher. You could compare it to the casting of a play; or perhaps to the arranging of an interesting marriage. From that, a great deal may follow automatically; but, as in human relation-ships, there is often the need for a measure of accommodation.

This is not a simple matter of limitation or restriction; the illustrator may find different aspects of his personality revealed or underlined by working with different authors and with different books. For me, this adaptation has proved to be one of the most enduringly interesting aspects of illustration, and I have been,

Tom lived with his maiden aunt, Miss Fidget Wonkham-Strong.
She wore an iron hat, and took no nonsense from anyone.
Where she walked the flowers drooped, and when she sang the
trees all shivered.

and still am, the partner in a variety of situations. The diversity of Dahl's books, for instance, makes them effective examples.

The first that I worked on was *The Enormous Crocodile.* It was also the first text that Dahl had written for a picture book. Its nature seems to give the illustrator some indications of how to set about it. It is a kind of pantomime story, and this crocodile is not exactly the crocodile of the real world. My ideas about it were as much influenced by the crocodile that used to appear, with clacking jaws, in the Punch and Judy show, as by a crocodile in the zoo. The teeth that I have drawn, for instance, look more like those of a saw than of any live creature. They are teeth for eating children with.

The pantomime mischief of the book seemed also to call for a rather harsh, almost diagrammatic kind of drawing. I generally use a rather scratchy writing pen nib to draw with, but for this I got something harder and squarer, which doesn't admit of neat details. In addition I incorporated the use of some concentrated watercolours; they're bright, almost luminous and give an almost heraldic quality to the pictures.

The next book that I did with Dahl was *The Twits*, and far from being in colour, it was very black, the black-and-whiteness of it very appropriate to the kind of story – comic, but with more than a hint of Samuel Beckett about it. My hard pen nib was still useful though, especially for Mr Twit's beard, which had to look like a lavatory brush.

Very often in a Dahl book there is an intrusive person who is the wicked one, such as the grandmother in *George's Marvellous Medicine* – but here it is almost a wicked world, or at least a wicked corner of the world, because the house and garden and life of the two Twits is all dark and it is the unfortunate little monkeys who live in the midst of it. The characters were not so difficult to establish, but I spent a long time drawing the house of the two Twits to get it to look as menacing and prison-like as possible.

From The Twits.

Roald Dahl's Revolting Rhymes offered a similar sort of problem; except that here the incidents are not new, but consist of mischievous, or as we might say nowadays, subversive retellings of familiar fairytales ornamented with a gamut of contemporary references and colloquialisms. The result is very funny but also farcical, abrasive and dark in mood. What I was also going to do was to try to suggest actions rather than actually show them; the use of what is sometimes referred to as "veiled menace". There was one exception to this, when the prince in Cinderella cuts off the head of one of the ugly sisters. It seemed unavoidable and irresistible, but I made sure there was no blood; the head comes off like a doorknob that might be fitted on again later. Even so, I believe there are children who have been frightened by the picture. Sorry about that.

This is a problem that I suppose every illustrator of children's books will come across from time to time: the Three Blind Mice situation. The writer (if anybody did once write that verse) can say "she cut off their tails with a carving knife" and, if you don't hang about, the thing is carried forward by the rhythm of the verse and no-one feels too bad about it. But consider the illustration! Consider all the possible ways of depicting the scene and how awful to contemplate how some of them could be... As an illustrator, you have to remember that you are in control of the situation, and do what is appropriate.

There are several such moments in *Revolting Rhymes*, on the part of both the author and the artist; the end of The Three Bears, for instance. First the author has Mother Bear suggest, teasingly, that as the Little Bear's breakfast is inside Goldilocks, the only way that he can get it back is by eating her. The illustration goes beyond the end of the story; not by showing the bear eating Goldilocks, but when he has done so. No unpleasant details; just the handkerchief wiping the mouth and the shoes and pigtail ribbons left behind on the carpet.

The Three Bears provides me with a diagrammatic example of adaptation, because I also drew them on another occasion. It was for a Japanese collection of folktales from the British Isles. Animals in human clothes would not have been appropriate there, because this story had to have a less specifically humorous approach – since it had also to accommodate other stories such as Mr Fox, an English version of the Bluebeard story – and I had to adopt a technique that could be used for all these situations.

It's this moving from mood to mood that has, all the more in recent years, afforded me an extra pleasure in the round of illustration tasks. Joan Aiken's *The Winter Sleepwalker* remains for me a striking example; a collection of invented folktales which mix traditional elements such as spells and witches and transformations with dustbins and rubber tyres and telephones, and in which the tone changes from story to story. Some of them are very funny indeed; others are gloomy and mysterious. When asked to supply a couple of sample drawings, I had no difficulty

The Three Bears and a moment from Mr Fox; *both from the Japanese collection* The True History of Sir Tom Thumb.

Opposite, from The Winter Sleepwalker.

Overleaf, illustration for the jacket of The Winter Sleepwalker.

in knowing which ones I wanted to try. First of all there was the horse with the eight legs and its sinister one-eyed rider galloping up the mountain track. And then, by contrast, the girl Alyss, playing her pipe in the woods in the story which gives the collection its name. Perhaps it was a sign of how excited I was that something quite extraordinary happened. It won't seem so if you have no experience of illustrating books, but it was extraordinary to me – the fact that both these pictures survived into the final book, where you can see them now. This almost never happens; there are nearly always some changes that have to be made to get

the pictures to fit together into a sequence. In fact I think there must have been some sort of charm on the book, because I did the cover in the same way – just did it once without discussing it with anyone, carried along on a smooth wave of euphoria. (Covers are normally the most difficult thing to do, and it is unusual not to have to make several attempts.)

However, enthusiasm for a project doesn't necessarily mean that its special problems will have easy solutions. One problem which belonged to *The Hunchback of Notre Dame* was that of scale. In my sample drawings I showed Quasimodo, the hunchback himself, in close-up, and satisfied myself at least about what he looked like; later, however, I had to make myself comfortable in a way of drawing that allowed me also to show quite crowded scenes, and even the whole façade of Notre Dame, when the two principal characters appear at its foot as tiny tweaks of the pen. There is also the question, for someone who draws in a convention that has its roots in caricature or exaggeration, of humour; of, more particularly, controlling it and keeping it in order. Part of this kind can be done by the nature of the drawing; the accuracy and nature of the delineation, the avoidance of broad effects.

Fortunately, it doesn't entail the eradication of humour altogether, because humour isn't a separate ingredient which you put into the cooking or leave out of it. It has much more to do with who you are and how you see things. Noting that, I realise that I have got to this point without so far saying anything specifically about humour. Strange, perhaps, since for many people that will be thought of as my main offering; but this not-mentioning-humour is no new experience for me, and on more than one occasion I have got to the end of a talk or interview only to realise that I had made no reference to it at all. I think this is perhaps because humour, insofar as you can identify it to talk about, is in some way a by-product; you produce it best almost by not thinking about it. Of course, after a while it's possible to learn a certain number of tactics or routines, as any experienced music-hall comedian or stand-up comic does – to signal reactions, for example, by putting in small spectators (mice and rabbits will do very well); or by making the pig's ears wave about expressively. But the essence is in the attitude of the illustrator.

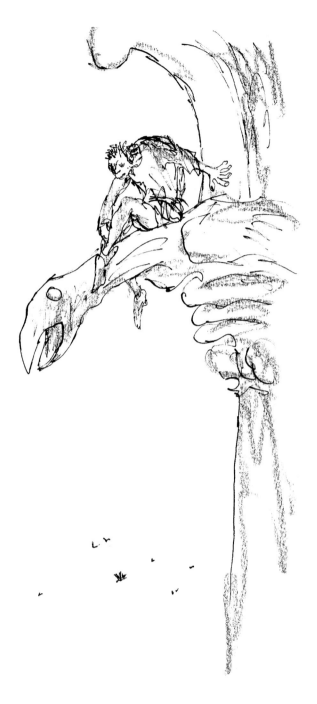

Facing, a full page and above a preliminary drawing for The Hunchback of Notre Dame.

The necessary thing is to concentrate on envisaging the situation. The incident may itself be funny, but even if it isn't intrinsically so, the humour will arise out of the way the situation is seen, the accuracy and idiosyncrasy of gesture and posture. And from that comes the satisfaction for the spectator, in touch as it were privately with the illustrator, of noting and savouring what is not said in the words.

I have illustrated other books in which humour is not the prevailing mode: I think of the French edition of Patricia MacLachlan's *Sarah Plain and Tall*, where sepia helped to establish the mood of the everydayness of times past; or a Puffin edition of *Huckleberry Finn*, a book which must always have been attractive to illustrators for the range of its possibilities. And these are not the only ones; but every book is in some sense a work of adaptation. My most extreme example of adaptation, and quite different, is *Monsters* by Russell Hoban, which deals with the drawings of a boy who likes drawing monsters. It seemed to me that it wasn't enough simply to look over the shoulder of the boy to see him drawing. I thought I actually ought to do the drawings myself; and so I had to learn once again how to do children's drawings.

Above, from Sarah Plain and Tall.
Facing page, from Huckleberry Finn.

I thought at first that I could do it by drawing with my left hand; but that gave me too little control. I had to practise having the desire to depict something, but at the same time to forego manipulative skill. I was also reminded that for children drawing a picture is an activity that exists in time – a happening – and as I tried for that I was soon close to making the noises that they make when they draw.

Of course, these drawings aren't truly children's drawings, because the creatures which I show very often have expressions or gestures which are disguised versions of what happens elsewhere in my own drawings. Nevertheless, it was fascinating to find my way back to the kind of drawing that you do when you are small. Once having got into it, I was taken with the habit and in fact I did far more drawings of this kind than were ever used in the book. One reviewer was later kind enough to observe that the drawings were "so good they might almost be by a child."

So far I have talked about the aspects of the illustrator's collaboration with the text; the ideas that it suggests to him and the adaptations it imposes. There is another set of constraints and one that doesn't directly stem from the writer's words: it is the question of the ways in which any set of illustrations has to be adapted to the format and extent of the final book.

This question of the way that illustration fits into the pages is one that has become steadily more interesting to me as I have done more books; the ways that there are of incorporating text and image together. It isn't absolutely necessary to do this, it has to be said: the great American illustrator Edward Gorey says quite simply, "text to the left, pictures to the right," and that's all there is to it. However I am sure that what he does have is a vision of the book as a whole; and it's this that an inexperienced illustrator, however talented, may sometimes have a problem in grasping. It's only too easy to be so taken up with the first illustration that you lose sight of whether the treatment is going to be appropriate to all the situations in the book; or to forget that the work of art is not the individual illustration but the entity of the book itself.

In my experience what the illustrator has to do is to start thinking in two directions at once: through the sequence of the pages as well as into the individual images. I also think that this is the most uncomfortable stage for the illustrator; for me it is, at any rate: the stage where nothing seems to come right, when you have doubts about whether you were right to take on this particular project, and when you wonder if you have finally lost whatever grasp you had of drawing ability. This is where the constraints – of colour, of format, of pagination – actually help to support you. You have to fulfill their requirements. Your first exploratory drawings begin silently to criticise each other. Eventually, it seems almost by accident, you do one that seems to offer the hint of a solution. The project begins to look possible once more.

I'm now well acquainted with this series of events, but looking back, I realise that it is something that must have been an unconscious concern when, for instance, about thirty years ago, I set about the illustration of *The Birds* of Aristophanes, for an edition to be published by the Lion and Unicorn Press, the private press of the Royal College of Art, in London. The play takes place in Cloud Cuckoo Land; there, the birds behave like people, and when the two main characters from Athens arrive they find themselves dressed up as birds. This world of Cloud Cuckoo Land is not described, and I didn't want to invent it. I wanted to keep the idea of a play, and for me the double page spread was a sort of empty stage. The characters come on to the page; there is text in relation to them but they walk on from the left or from the right. A feathered messenger swoops in from above; the Goddess Iris is lowered from the top of the page as the *dea ex machina* to bring her message which concludes the play. I found that I was treating the page as an open area where the characters, in fancy-dress, act out the story. I think this approach – the page as being the place where the story happens – has been in the back of my mind ever since.

over men, but the Birds. Let me cite you a few proofs.
Consider the Cock.
Long before any Dareioses or Megabazoses
the Cock was King of the Persians, and such a king
that ever since he's been called the Persian Bird.

Euelpides That's why, even now,
Cocks strut like the Shah; and of all birds living
only they have a right to the tiara.

*A double page
spread from*
The Birds *of
Aristophanes.*

Pisthetairos   What power he had! Why, to this very day
                when the Cock sings at dawn
                everyone jumps out of bed and goes to work:
                blacksmiths, potters, tanners, shoemakers,
                grocers, masseurs, lyre-&-shield-manufacturers –
                Some of them are hard at it before it's light.

The exercises of the best dancing-master
are out of place in chemistry.

It is impossible to embrace the
unembraceable.

If you want to be beautiful, join
the Hussars.

Nails and hair are given to man for
constant and easy occupation

Do not joke with women; such jokes are
foolish and indecent.

Most books, needless to say, don't present you with such a diagrammatic situation. The layout of a book is most complicated when there is both a lot of text and a large number of illustrations which have to be reconciled with each other. (A picture book is rather different, because often the text is so short that it can easily sit next to, or be tucked into, the illustrations, which in themselves form the shape of the book.) There are different ways of setting about this job. One is for the illustrator to be commissioned to do a certain number of drawings. When they are completed they are handed over to a designer employed by the publisher who fits them together with the text. The more drawings there are the harder it is for him to keep them the right size and in the right place. Another way is for the designer to lay out the text leaving gaps for the illustrations in what he thinks are the appropriate places. With this method the illustrator may sometimes want to ask if the text can be shunted this way or that to make room for a picture that needs extra space. All this is done better if there is a good collaborative understanding between the

illustrator and the designer. Even so, it seems to me that there are often decisions left to the designer which could, or ought to be, taken by the illustrator; so that what I particularly like is to be given a set of galley-proofs or print-outs of the text. With scissors and tape and photocopies of the roughs, I stick everything together myself in exactly the position I want it. Not only can the pictures fall just where you need them, but they can be drawn to fit; you avoid the situation where the designer is faced with no recourse but to enlarge or reduce your drawing because there is too much or too little space.

Featherbrains by John Yeoman is a good example of a book that benefits from being treated in this way. It's the story of two battery chickens who accidentally escape from their prison, and (eventually) come to terms with the dangers and embarrassments of liberty with the assistance of a shrewd and helpful jackdaw. The drawings give a blow-by-blow account of their adventures which keeps pace with the words; you have to make sure that both versions appear side-by-side on every page.

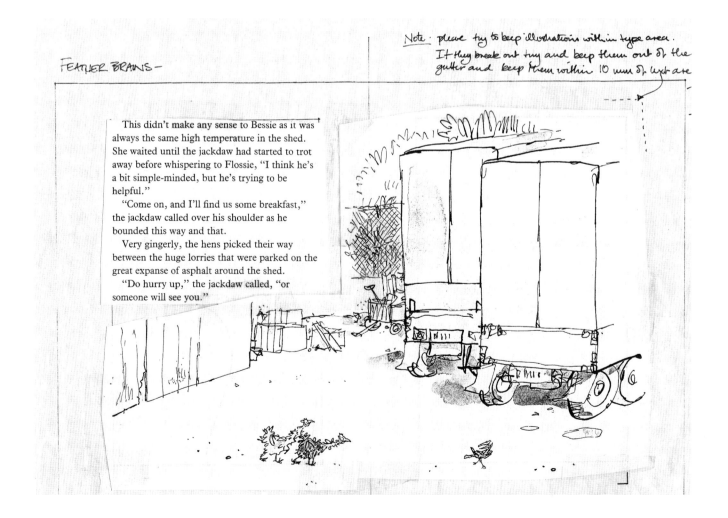

Roald Dahl's *Esio Trot* offers an even more complicated variant. The story is almost entirely played out in the restricted surroundings of two apartments; that of Mr Hoppy upstairs, with his balcony crowded with plants, and that of Mrs Silver downstairs, with her balcony on which lives Alfie, her tortoise, in his little house. There are only one or two other scenes: and so the illustrator who is arranging the pages finds himself rather in the position of a director making a film of a play. Every camera angle has to be used, the balconies from above and below, the different corners of the room, longshot and close-up, and the cast of tortoises who play such an important part in the plot disposed in various ways. You need that wide picture (I remember Roald Dahl pointing out to me the advantage of it) with the floor encumbered with tortoises stretching away in all directions; and the tall pictures to show the tortoise-catcher descending to catch hold of the astonished Alfie.

In recent years I have got to depend on this layout procedure, and have become so used to doing it that I can now normally arrange the text and tape it down without doing any drawings at all but simply imagining what I would like to draw and leaving the

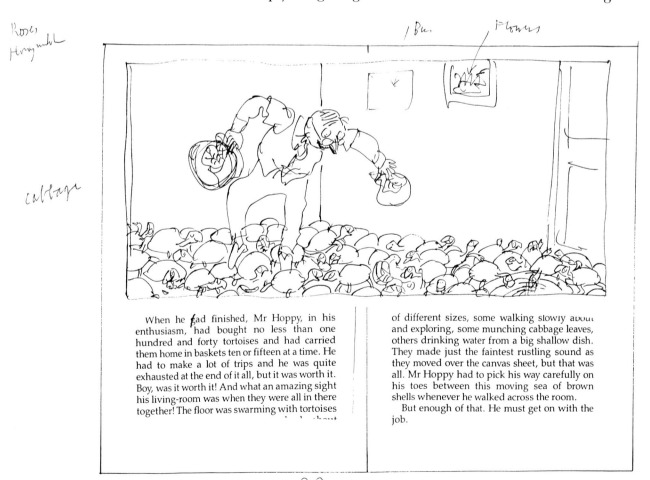

When he fad finished, Mr Hoppy, in his enthusiasm, had bought no less than one hundred and forty tortoises and had carried them home in baskets ten or fifteen at a time. He had to make a lot of trips and he was quite exhausted at the end of it all, but it was worth it. Boy, was it worth it! And what an amazing sight his living-room was when they were all in there together! The floor was swarming with tortoises

of different sizes, some walking slowly about and exploring, some munching cabbage leaves, others drinking water from a big shallow dish. They made just the faintest rustling sound as they moved over the canvas sheet, but that was all. Mr Hoppy had to pick his way carefully on his toes between this moving sea of brown shells whenever he walked across the room.

But enough of that. He must get on with the job.

appropriate space for it; and then, later, with everything in position, going on to the illustrations themselves. All this activity of reading and snipping and arrangement is, as I've explained, a necessary process for me. It also has the advantage of providing a sort of ballast to the daily life of the studio; an element of hand work especially useful since nothing in the actual drawing process is done slowly – there is no steady work of cross-hatching or colouring-in – and I need something to provide calm intervals of reflection.

Nearly every morning I go into the room that I use as a studio. It looks out from the second floor at the trees of a Kensington square. In the room are bookshelves; shelves carrying paper and materials; three plan-chests; a guillotine; a table with a lightbox where I stand to draw; another table at right angles to it covered with watercolour materials; a tall movable chair; a coffee table, and a swivel armchair where I sit between bursts of drawing. There are books and papers everywhere. I don't wait for inspiration. I'm not, in fact, quite sure what inspiration is, but I'm sure that if it is going to turn up, my having started work is the precondition of its arrival.

Fortunately, there is nearly always some task waiting to be attempted, and I only stop drawing if I am doing it very badly and the effect is counterproductive. I try to stay near the work, even if not much is happening. I remember that in the years when I was teaching it would sometimes take, on the first morning back in the studio, up to lunchtime or even till four o'clock in the afternoon before enough readjustment had taken place, enough energy had worked itself back into the mind and fingers, for anything worthwhile to happen.

If I have a spare engagement diary I try to remember to write very brief notes of what I did each day. I generally fail to keep it up for a whole year and months go by when I forget all about it; in fact the only whole complete year I can discover is 1993. I was already five years free of commitments to the Royal College of Art and for that reason, and also perhaps just coincidentally, it was probably one of the busiest years I have spent; I choose it, however, not for that reason but simply because it exists and I think that it gives an idea of the mixture of elements that make up for me a year of illustration.

Obviously the work that a book entails doesn't arrange itself neatly into a calendar year; but I see that in this year I finished off *Simpkin* and did most of the work on:

Roald Dahl's *Danny, The Champion of the World*

Joan Aiken's *The Winter Sleepwalker*

One section of the collected *Cautionary Verses* by Hilaire Belloc

The Do-It-Yourself House that Jack Built, a picture book by John Yeoman, and (rather surprisingly because we generally do just one book a year together) a collection of stories, *The Singing Tortoise,* and verses, *The Family Album.*

Polissena del Porcello by Bianca Pitzorno, for the Italian publisher Mondadori; a story about a girl who escapes from a nunnery carrying a piglet and joins a group of children and animals in a wandering Commedia del Arte company.

Quentin Blake Agenda – an illustrated diary for the Dutch publishers, Fontein, with words by John Yeoman, and drawings of different activities for each month of the year.

I also did the first roughs for *Clown,* and the cover design and two sample drawings for *Don Quixote* which I would be illustrating in the following year for The Folio Society. At the same time I was collecting poems and writing the introduction for *The Penguin Book of Nonsense Verse.*

This is the cat
        that killed the rat
            that ate the malt
                that lay in the house
                    that Jack built.

This is the cat that killed the rat that ate the malt that
lay in the house that Jack built.

Lower left is John Yeoman's original rough for
The Do-It-Yourself House that Jack Built;
on the right my version of it and, above, the final pages.

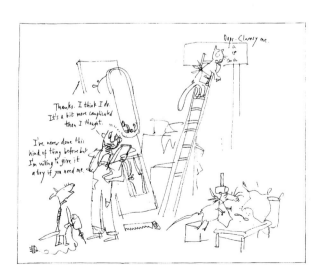

Frequently projects that have been completed don't allow themselves to be set aside and forgotten about; there is an element of after-sales service. So that in this year I also tinted the black and white illustrations to three books for coloured French editions, and did new jackets for four Roald Dahl books for Puffin Books. I also had to draw the sets and some new characters for Joan Aiken's Arabel and Mortimer stories which were being made into an animated series for television. Before the year began I had completed a set of five Christmas stamps based on Charles Dickens' *A Christmas Carol*, and Selfridges department store in Oxford Street had arranged with the Royal Mail to produce huge three-dimensional versions; as there were more than five windows more drawings had to be done for those. It's also an unusual year that doesn't include the illustration of one or two Christmas cards (quite often, it seems, to be done in the hottest days of August) and this year there were the Royal Mail (*A Christmas Carol* again), The London Library, the Musicians' Benevolent Fund, the Royal College of Art and a green Father Christmas for David Mellor, the designer.

There were also a poster for the Unicorn Theatre; a drawing for the Friends of the Earth; one for *The Times Educational Supplement* for a Dahl feature; and a full-colour Toucan for a teeshirt for the charity Survival.

A carrier bag illustrated specially for Selfridges.

From Polissena del Porcello.

From My Year.

*Opposite, an illustrated teeshirt
for the charity* Survival.

Quentin Blake

ROYAL MAIL MINT STAMPS

The five Christmas Carol stamps for the Royal Mail.

*Christmas cards for The Royal College of Art,
The RSA and The London Library.*

In addition to this, there were two or three book reviews, and two or three interviews. There were also, unusual for any year, two exhibitions. One was of oil paintings and watercolour drawings done in the years since I had given up teaching; a continuation of that vein of pictures, already mentioned, that I have kept on with intermittently since my time at Chelsea. The other was my first exhibition at Chris Beetles' Gallery. It was devoted to work related to the books of Roald Dahl. It came about initially because I was looking for a way of selling a clutch of watercolour drawings left over from *My Year* for the benefit of the Roald Dahl Foundation. That did indeed happen, because Chris Beetles was ready to put on the show. However, when I asked how many pieces of work he felt he would need, he said, "About a hundred and fifty," so that I had to institute a search through portfolios and plan-chest drawers and the show became one for me as well as for the Foundation. (All the originals were related to books but had not actually appeared in them.)

The year also included a handful of visits. One was to join Brian Alderson at the Children's Book Conference of the University of Southern Mississippi, where I gave a talk about where ideas come from and was given a bronze medallion. Another was to the town of Montaubon in South West France at the invitation of the local libraries' service, who were taking a group of writers and artists to speak in local schools and libraries. Wonderful to cross those French playgrounds and find all the pictures and cut-out models of the Enormous Crocodile, and have the children singing their song about him. It was here too that I was given a flight-feather from a French vulture which I cut into a quill. Vultures seemed to be exactly the thing to draw with it.

Since then one or more visits to France have been a feature of every year; which serves also to underline the fact that nowadays any illustrator, and in particular an illustrator of children's books, can well be international; not least because the economic viability of books produced expensively in colour depends on the existence of co-editions. For the author and illustrator too, of course, the co-edition is the most profitable way of producing a book. Despite this I find it hard to resist the direct commission from a foreign publisher, even with small prospects of parallel editions, just for the interest of the thing. So that *Polissena* in my 1993 list is one of a number of books by the Italian writer Bianca Pitzorno which I have done for Mondadori. Commissions from

A continuation of Mrs Armitage drawn to the instructions of French school children and, right, self-portraits in the kitchen, also to instruction.

France present no serious language problem as I can read French sufficiently well to cope; commissions from Italy are rather strange as I don't speak Italian, so that I have to work from a list of suggestions and get some friendly Italian-speaker to compare my roughs with the original text. We manage. With the USA there is also no language problem, and even working at such long distances seems not to be a difficulty, perhaps because it requires everyone to be specific, so that confusions are avoided. And we have couriers, and the fax machine; so that, for instance, I have recently, between South Kensington and San Diego, discovered the pleasures of Edward Eager, that lively American disciple of E. Nesbit, for whose books I have re-illustrated the jackets; and have had the pleasure of creating a California-style talking clothes moth for *The Emperor's New Clothes*, a star-studded retelling of the story, (by Harrison Ford, Madonna, Norman Schwarzkopf and others) for the Starbright Foundation, the children's charity of which Steven Spielberg is the Chairman; as well as producing a book about how to draw, designed especially for people who think they are no good at drawing, for the inimitable Klutz press in Palo Alto.

Above and right, the moth from
The Emperor's New Clothes.

The Time Garden

Half Magic

Cover illustrations for books by Edward Eager.

Knight's Castle

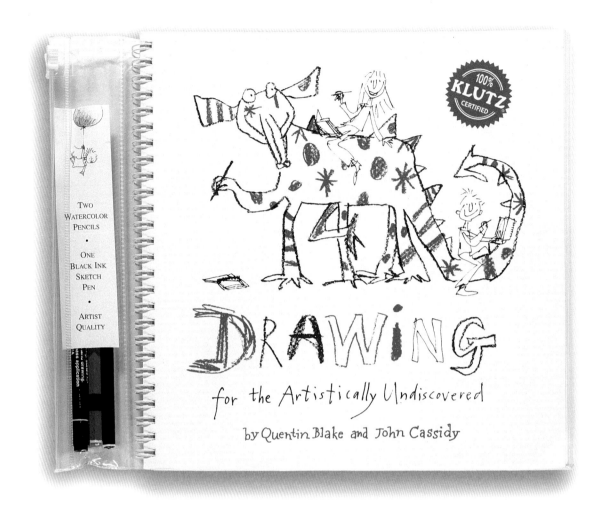

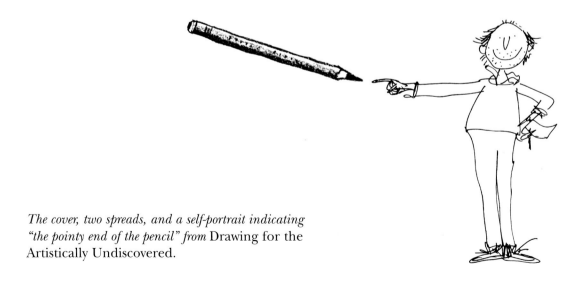

The cover, two spreads, and a self-portrait indicating "the pointy end of the pencil" from Drawing for the Artistically Undiscovered.

Dealing with Human Anatomy (OUR WAY)

The anatomy we show here is not right — but it's not wrong either. If you decide to add more detail later, you won't need to unlearn anything from these pages. And neither forget nor despair: Sins of botched details will all be forgiven if you can catch an essential bit of posture or gesture.

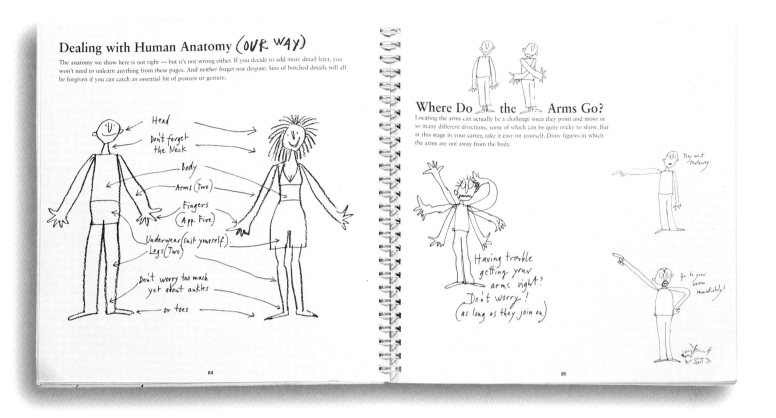

Head
Don't forget the Neck
Body
Arms (Two)
Fingers (App. Five)
Underwear (suit yourself)
Legs (Two)
Don't worry too much yet about ankles
or toes

Where Do the Arms Go?

Locating the arms can actually be a challenge since they point and move in so many different directions, some of which can be quite tricky to show. But at this stage in your career, take it easy on yourself. Draw figures in which the arms are out away from the body.

Having trouble getting your arms right? Don't worry! (as long as they join on.)

They went that way.

Go to your room immediately!

84

85

Probably Your Very First Procession

Finish all these drawings, not forgetting to use your red pencil. Sign your work when you're finished, please.

The three-legged four-headed Murgle

The giant goofy daisy

The long-eared Moon Rabbit

The Hairy Dog

Marvo the Amazing Balancing Act

Ermintrude and her Umbrella

100

101

Books and activities of this kind, even if they don't always run at the level of my sample year of 1993, create the need for an extraordinary amount of communication – letters, faxes, phone calls. It would be more than I could cope with myself and for twenty years now I have had help for two or three days a week: help to pack and send drawings and (more difficult) to get them back later; to send messages to say that I can or (more likely) cannot accept the invitation to the school's book week; to send thanks for the unsolicited manuscript and to explain that there is no possibility of my illustrating it; to apologise for the fact that I cannot fill up students' questionnaires and to send some newspaper cuttings which may provide some answers nonetheless; to send thanks for children's letters and say how much I like their drawings (I really do like their drawings); to keep track of exhibitions; to organise invitation lists; and then, beyond that, all the day to day detail of bills, taxes, income.

I am grateful to have faithful supporters who can cope with all this, and more than grateful to be in business as an illustrator, though there are times when it seems strangely different from the early days when I first started to sell drawings and my records consisted entirely of a little cash book which, if I was lucky, had two or three entries on the page devoted to the current month:

Punch	£7 7s 0d
Spectator	£8 0s 0d

It's evident that drawing is the basis of everything I do; it took me some time to come to terms with colour, and I feel that I'm still finding out about it now. But perhaps one is always finding out about colour.

At the end of the fifties *Punch* magazine decided to have a new cover each week. (For a hundred and fifty years before that, they had used the same cover, a much-loved drawing by Dicky Doyle, simply changing the date each week). A number of the covers I submitted were accepted and it proved to be a useful opportunity for experiment, because the cover-artist has only to discover a visual solution that will work once and doesn't have to be repeated. (Unlike a book, where you have to establish a technique for its complete continuity.) The first of my covers, of

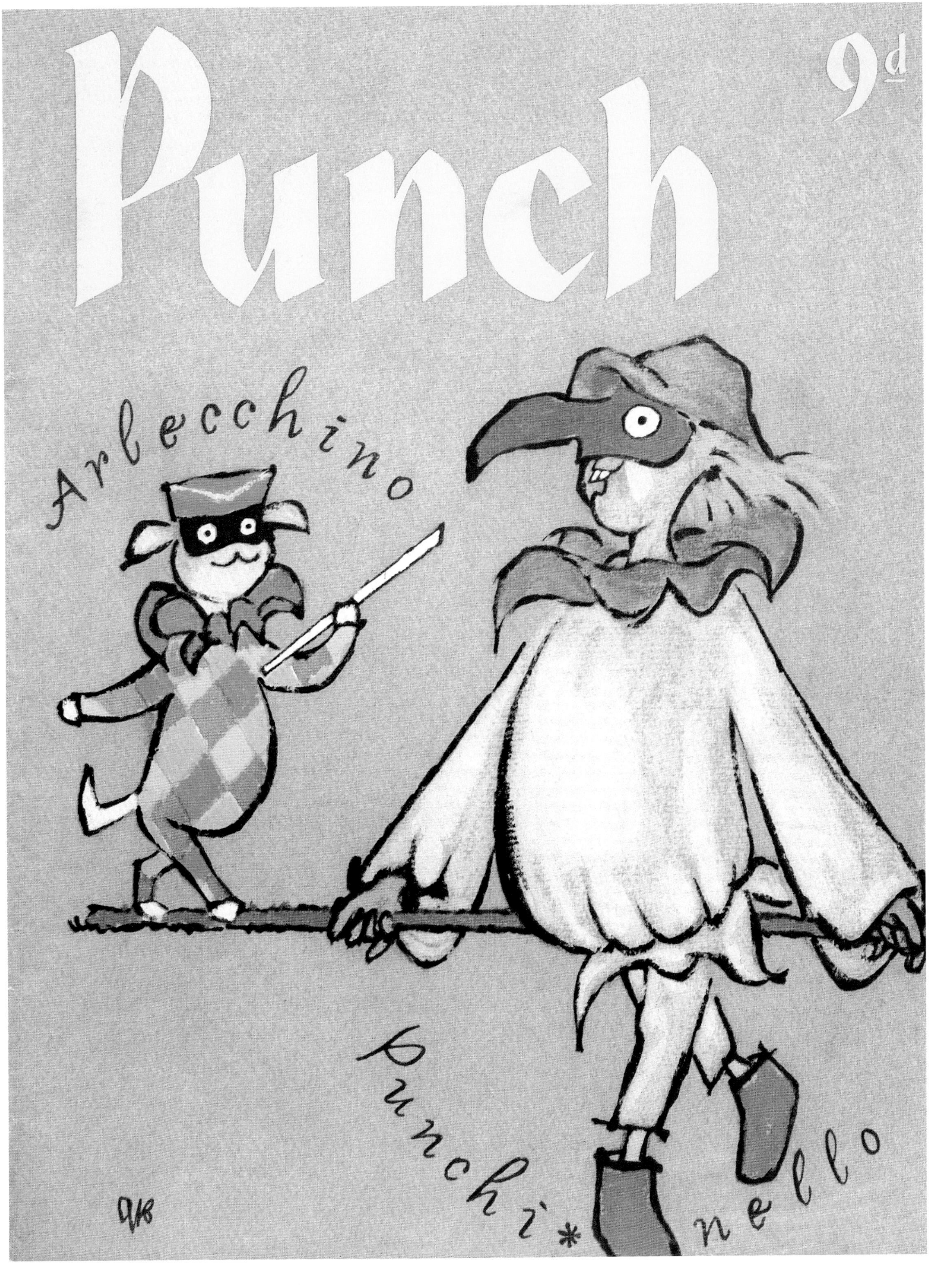
Punch
9d
Arlecchino
Punchi*nello

Punch as Punchinello and dog Toby as Harlequin, was an experiment in the sense that anything I had done at that time would have been an experiment, such was my inexperience. The picture was drawn on Ingres paper with a plastic toothpick (as near as I could get to a quill at the time – they are rather good to draw with) and coloured in with blackboard chalks. They were the things that I happened to have to hand. For subsequent covers I made an intentional effort to vary my materials: pastels, oil pastels, watercolour pastels, coloured inks, wrapping paper – even the glass eyes supplied for the repair of teddy bears. What calls for more, if less evident, effort is to experiment with colour itself. I can draw without a sense of inhibition; but it took me a long time to get over a certain prejudice that the leaves of trees are green and that their trunks are brown and

that the sky is blue, though to the eye they may be blue or purple or brown. The arrival of bad weather in a picture is always a help; and sometimes even willfully to introduce arbitrary colours may help me to realise that perhaps they are not quite so arbitrary after all.

Another question to be resolved, particularly where narrative is concerned, is the relationship between line and colour: it's quite common to find them in competition with each other, and you have to decide the balance of power between them. With me, it is mainly the line that is bearing the message, and for a long time now my favourite medium to accompany it has been watercolour. I like its lightness and fluidity; the brush has its own gestural quality, and the brushmarks don't have to fit the forms they are colouring. There's nothing to encumber movement. There is,

nevertheless, an enormous amount that even a discreet use of colour can add by way of mood and atmosphere.

Lightness and fluidity isn't, of course, the only possible effect. *The Enormous Crocodile,* as I've already mentioned, needed a relatively strong, sharp treatment, with some of the extra zing that the more intense colour of inks can give.

Perhaps strangely, *Roald Dahl's Revolting Rhymes* turned out to be at the opposite end of this spectrum. The first intention was to illustrate the book in black and white; which seemed to make sense, since there is more than a hint of darkness in the way these verses reveal the truth behind familiar fairytales, and it was this which led me to add shading with a litho crayon to enhance the effect. Later, however, other counsels prevailed, and it was decided to publish the book in colour nonetheless. When I say later, I mean just when I had finished all the drawings. There was a queasy interval in which I was unable to think of a way of converting these essentially black and white images to colour and contemplated the prospect of starting the whole project over again from scratch. Then I remembered the tinted versions I had seen of nineteenth century prints – lithographs by Daumier and Gavarni. Perhaps my drawings would also accept those pale washes of watercolour. I photocopied the illustrations on to more sheets of watercolour paper and experimented. Though this isn't at all the recommended way of setting about a book, I think the emergency gave me a set of pictures that were more interesting than they would have been if I had set out from the start to produce illustrations in colour.

Perhaps it was because of this experience that, when I came to illustrate a picture book selection of Hilaire Belloc's Cautionary Verses under the title *Algernon* I had deliberate recourse to the illustration techniques of earlier times. Because they were such large simple pictures – a lion eating a small boy, a man in a top hat hitting his nephew with an umbrella, and so on – it seemed that I had the opportunity to use some strong colour, and I wanted it to be reminiscent of the printing of a hundred years ago when these little parodies of moral tales were written. I'm not exactly sure how the popular picture books and magazines of that time were printed, but the effect was of overprinting in the tradition of lithography. I wanted something that looked like that, despite the fact that that is not the way picture books are

From Roald Dahl's Revolting Rhymes.

Three threatening moments from Algernon *by Hilaire Belloc.*

George,

Who played with a Dangerous Toy,
and suffered a Catastrophe of Considerable Dimensions.

When George's Grandmamma was told
That George had been as good as Gold,
She Promised in the Afternoon
To buy him an *Immense BALLOON.*

And so she did; but when it came,
It got into the candle flame,

printed nowadays, and after a bit of experiment I discovered a method using concentrated watercolours and painting (instead of printing) one on top of another while they are still wet; so that green is actually yellow painted on to blue, with a little edge where the colours don't quite meet which suggests an inaccuracy of registration in the printing. It's also exciting to do, because as you do it you're guessing the result, or at least trying to control it by the quantity of each colour on the brush; and you have the chance of finding colours that you (or at least I) might not have imagined, like the fatally threatening darkness of George's Enormous Balloon.

There is no mistaking the fact that colour is an important aspect of the picture story book; but in order to say more about how these books come into being, and in some respects what they are for, I need to look back at the earliest picture books of my own devising. The first of these, *Patrick*, appeared just over thirty years ago. I can very well remember what I saw as its *raison d'être*: up to that point, no publisher (despite my work for *Punch* and *The Spectator*) had been ready to take a chance on commissioning me to work in colour. So what I had to produce – I realised at last, with an extraordinary slowness of apprehension – was a story that had to be in colour. Hence this story of a young man who buys a second-hand violin which, when you play it, has the magical effect of (thank goodness) making things change colour – and a number of other unexpected results (stars, feathers, sparks, cream buns and slices of hot buttered toast) for good measure. It was drawn in Indian ink on ready-mounted Saunders watercolour paper, and the longed-for colour added in the form of watercolour, coloured ink, and, most enjoyable for me, watercolour pastels. Tom Maschler, publisher of this book as of so many subsequent ones, was resolute in ensuring that, although I had a tendency to tighten up the drawing as the final stages approached, it should remain properly relaxed. One of the things a good publisher can do, like a good teacher, is to help the artist find his own best way of doing things.

Patrick was followed by *Jack and Nancy*, which was about stormy weather and tropical colour; *Angelo*, which was about tightrope walking (and therefore balance), and *Commedia del Arte* costumes: and *Snuff*, in which the small hero was page to Sir

From Patrick.

And so the three went down the road together.
Soon they came to an orchard of apple trees. Patrick
played his violin and the leaves on the trees changed
to all kinds of bright colours.

Instead of apples the trees began to grow pears and
bananas and cakes and ice-creams and slices of hot
buttered toast. Kath and Mick ran about among the
trees and helped themselves to whatever they liked.

Up they went through the clouds...

From Jack and Nancy.

Thomas Magpie, a sort of harmless version of Falstaff. It was the Elizabethan accessories and the contrast between their two figures that got me started. Unfortunately, they couldn't also get me finished and I had to rely on John Yeoman to rescue me. He silently rewrote the second half of the story; and the Boot Thieves and their undoing were entirely his work (with inspiration from the silent film actor, Max Linder).

Each of these four books had its origin in a little clutch of images and not essentially in the story, which was something added to the pictures. I don't mean that the stories were failures – at least the books have been more or less continuously in print ever since – but, although their simplicity was important, perhaps they were not sufficiently ingenious; or, as Brian Alderson has suggested, they didn't quite give the reader the sense of their being inevitable. At any rate, I came to realise that they did not offer a way ahead. New ideas and new approaches were needed. But where were they to come from?

And so Angelo and Angelina danced together on the rope, and the people laughed and clapped to see them wherever they went.

From Angelo.

From Snuff.

We approach that favourite question asked of writers and artists: Where do you get your ideas from? I have two answers to this question. One refers to my own books, and very roughly speaking it amounts to: "I don't know." However, I think there are things that it is possible to do to encourage ideas, and with me that may mean sitting and thinking about things I enjoy drawing, or perhaps looking at some of my old drawings. In the seventies, for instance, I did several shows at Mel Calman's Workshop Gallery which were of pictures done specially for exhibition, and, like that, I found several themes that were useful later – women riding bicycles, or dancing with birds; pigs and parrots; various kinds of music; and so on. There may still be some that I may yet come to – I remember there were a number of rather scruffy men who seemed to be owl-fanciers in the way that some people are pigeon-fanciers. Sadly, I never found their meaning or their story. I had better luck with some pictures of people wheeling birds in push-chairs, which have come together with some old pictures of women cosseting their pets, and occasionally their men, and which bid fair to emerge one day as another picture book.

The second answer to the question, "Where do you get your ideas from?" is: from authors. There are two advantages for an illustrator of working with other people's texts. One is that you are led into subjects and situations that you didn't know you could deal with; didn't yet know you liked. The second is that you are introduced to a variety of ways of looking at and thinking about narrative and presentation. What could be more educational, for example, than setting to work on Russell Hoban's *How Tom Beat Captain Najork and his Hired Sportsmen?* Just to receive the three or four pages of typescript was in itself a revivifying experience: to discover a story that you feel had come into existence especially for you, full of things that you wished you would have imagined if you had had the imagination to do so. It begins in a way that is marked by that gift some writers seem mysteriously to possess, authority of statement.

"Tom lived with his maiden aunt, Miss Fidget Wonkham Strong. She wore an iron hat, and took no nonsense from anyone."

These striking metaphorical statements – the iron hat, the hired sportsmen who contrast so pathetically with Tom and his experienced spontaneity – build into a fable about the nature of education (doesn't the flavour include a tinge of *Hard Times*, and *Huckleberry Finn?*) where everything is manifest in wonderful performance. I was taken by surprise a second time, because I would have thought that a sequel to such a complete work would have been impossible. But the sequel is brilliantly conceived in what is fundamentally a different convention, even though it is visually the same. It's farce, by which I don't mean that it is simply exaggerated but that it is organised in the theatre convention of farce, where two or more sequences of activity proceed independently, interlocking at unexpected moments.

A rough for the cover of A Near Thing for Captain Najork.

Facing page, above from How Tom Beat Captain Najork and His Hired Sportsmen, *and below,* A Near Thing for Captain Najork.

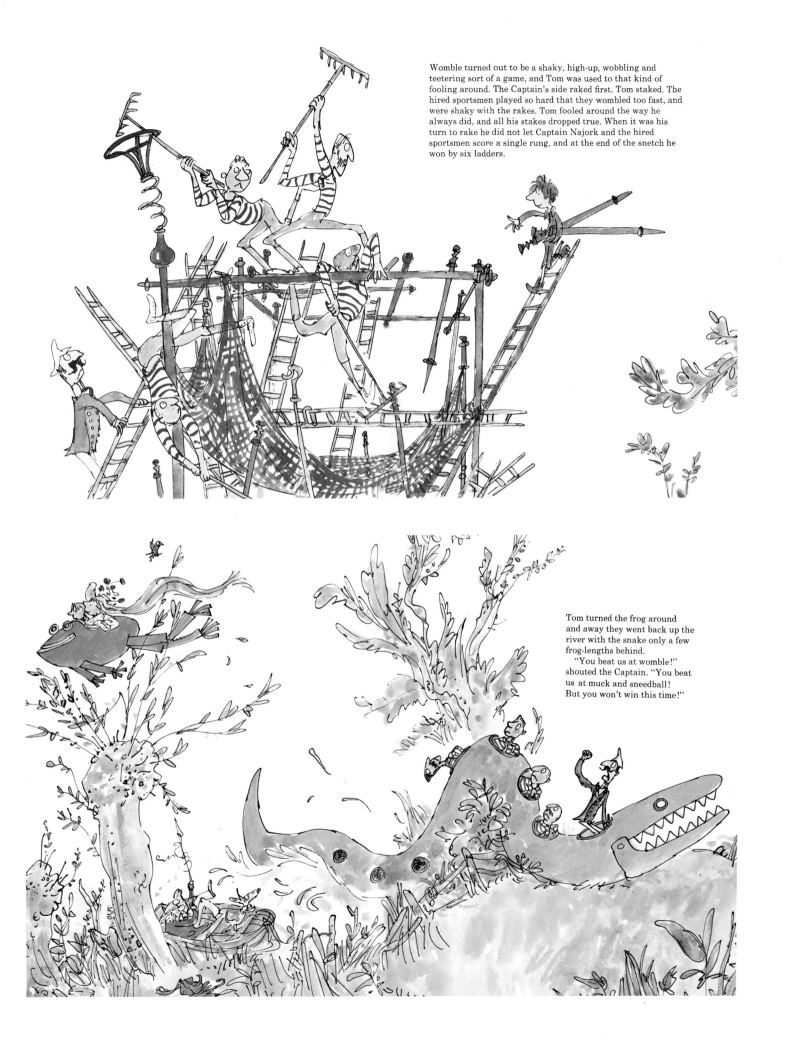

Womble turned out to be a shaky, high-up, wobbling and teetering sort of a game, and Tom was used to that kind of fooling around. The Captain's side raked first. Tom staked. The hired sportsmen played so hard that they wombled too fast, and were shaky with the rakes. Tom fooled around the way he always did, and all his stakes dropped true. When it was his turn to rake he did not let Captain Najork and the hired sportsmen score a single rung, and at the end of the snetch he won by six ladders.

Tom turned the frog around and away they went back up the river with the snake only a few frog-lengths behind.

"You beat us at womble!" shouted the Captain. "You beat us at muck and sneedball! But you won't win this time!"

My horizons of possibility had been enlarged even earlier by another river-ry experience, which Brian Alderson identified as "the one fine pointer to the future" amongst my early work: John Yeoman's *Sixes and Sevens*. This is what he had to say of it in *The Horn Book*:

> *The unfazable hero is Barnaby, setting out on a raft to Limber Lea, and remembering to look in his big box when difficulties threaten. This they do in profusion as he poles down-river picking up first one kitten, then two mice, then three school mistresses (almost like the twelve days of Christmas). The big box does indeed yield help: a sock to put the kitten in, a jam-jar for the mice, but a succession of schoolboys, monkeys, parrots and dogs bring wild confusion. In the midst of which Barnaby plies his raft with a sublime – and finally justified – certainty that all will be well. Yeoman's text is not just a neat version of a cumulative counting story: it is also spiced from incident to incident with rhyming quatrains which help to give shape and character to the text, and the potential of the whole thing for high farce inspired Blake to a degree of graphic sportiveness that is not present in his own early picture books.*

There was also a third project which had an effect on the development of my work. I was asked to illustrate a book by Dr Seuss, called *Great Day for Up!* There was more than one curiosity about this venture. To begin with, when Dr Seuss wrote to be illustrated by others he used the name Theo Leseig (a rearrangement of the rest of his name: he was Theodore Seuss Geisel) but this book was by Dr Seuss. I never really discovered why he wasn't ready to illustrate this book himself – perhaps he just couldn't face dealing with the multiplicity of characters that he had written into the last two or three double-page spreads – but it came somewhere between the two types, in that my illustrations were based on his roughs. This may sound like a recipe for discord, but the whole thing took place easily, with the master in La Jolla asking for no more correction than a little adjustment to the necks of a pair of giraffes.

The additional reward of the project, however, was the insight given me by collaborating with such an old hand at the game. The text worked perfectly – you could jump up and down on it and it wouldn't collapse – and being jumped up and down on is

Opposite: two spreads from Great Day for Up! *Overleaf: original illustration and layout for* Sixes and Sevens.

UP!

Up, voices!
Louder! Higher!

Great day
to sing
up on a wire.

UP! UP! UP!

Great day for UP!

Wake every person,
pig and pup,
till EVERYONE
on Earth is up!

3

Next he stopped at Parson's Barrow
and was met by Felicity Parfitt:

'Three schoolmistresses, stiff as twigs,'
    she said,
'As quiet as quiet can be.
But the mice will get in their wigs,'
    she said,
'From here to Limber Lea.'

So Barnaby looked in his big box
to see what he could see,
and he pulled out a jam-jar.
'The mice can stay in the jam-jar from here
to Limber Lea,' he said,
'and then I won't have any difficulties.'

what, metaphorically at least, happens to the words of children's picture books: they are made for constant repetition. Even more than that, Dr Seuss's books have a wonderful gift of nonsense and awareness of the possibilities of language. *Great Day for Up!* is all about Up – up in the morning, up on stilts, up in balloons – and though it has a shape, it isn't a story. I think it must have been working on this book that got it into my head at last that a picture book doesn't have to be a straightforward recounted narrative.

The fruit of this enlightenment, and what felt like a fresh start, was *Mr Magnolia*. The simple nonsense rhyming verse and the counting-book structure allowed me to delve into the hamper of things which are fun to draw: dancing, juggling, playing the trumpet; parakeets, owls, a dinosaur. The rhyme bolted it together. *Simpkin* works in much the same way. It starts off as one of those books which exist to teach children ideas – concepts – such as high and low and inside and outside, and quickly goes off the rails. The words don't mean much without the pictures, and the pictures are telling you, in addition, something about family relationships.

*Left, drawings from which came the idea of
Mr Magnolia and, right, an early version of the story.*

Mr Magnolia has only
one boot

He has a red trumpet
that goes rooty-toot

But Mr Magnolia has
only one boot

He will dance for his aunts
when they play on the flute

There are lovely green patches
sewn on to his suit

He has some fat owls who are learning to hoot

He takes all his friends
when he goes for a scoot

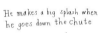

He makes a big splash when
he goes down the chute

His favourite trick is
to juggle with fruit

When the mice all march
past he can take the
salute —

And his dinosaur is
a MAGNIFICENT brute!

But Mr Magnolia
— poor Mr Magnolia —
Mr Magnolia has only
one boot

And that's all

Having moved away from the idea of setting about a story directly allowed me eventually to get back into it. At any rate *The Story
of the Dancing Frog* was written more in the spirit of something produced by a writer (that is to say you can just about read it without
the pictures) than anything so far. I even have some memories of
where the idea came from. A few years before I had given a lec-
ture to an audience of teachers and librarians and I wanted to
make a point about some of the things that can happen to drawing when it becomes illustration. To do that I needed some small
creature that could be drawn, quite quickly, in front of the audience. I settled almost at random for a frog. First I drew it as nat-
uralistically as possible in the time available; and then I drew it
doing something that doesn't happen in nature but which might
happen in a book – dancing. (One of the special abilities of
Beatrix Potter, incidentally, was to combine both these ways of
drawing in the same picture; just look, for instance, at *The Tale of
Two Bad Mice.*)

After the conference the dancing frog stayed with me in some
corner of my mind and perhaps would never have got into a book
at all if it hadn't got mixed up with some other thoughts from my
experience as a teacher of illustration, about the problems and
consolations that could be found in art by women who had
embraced that career. The way the story is told – as a story within
a story – also led me to think about the value and use of stories
(whether true or not) and to experience a miniature insight into
the fascination of having someone else tell the story: that
Unreliable Narrator which has been of such interest to so many
writers since Chaucer, who no doubt did it best of all. In the first
reviews no-one seemed to have noticed any of this; but there is
now a book for school use (a collection of "photocopiable activities") which is aware of these considerations and uses them as a
basis for enquiry and discussion.

The idea of stories about our forebears helped to set me off on
the frog's adventures in the theatre. I remembered my father
once mentioning that, when my parents lived in France in the
twenties, before I was born, they had been to the theatre and
seen a lady who danced wearing nothing but a string of bananas.
Later on I realised that this could only have been Josephine
Baker; and so her meeting with the frog was for me an essential
foundation stone in the making of the book. As it happened, the
prospective publishers in the USA said that they would not

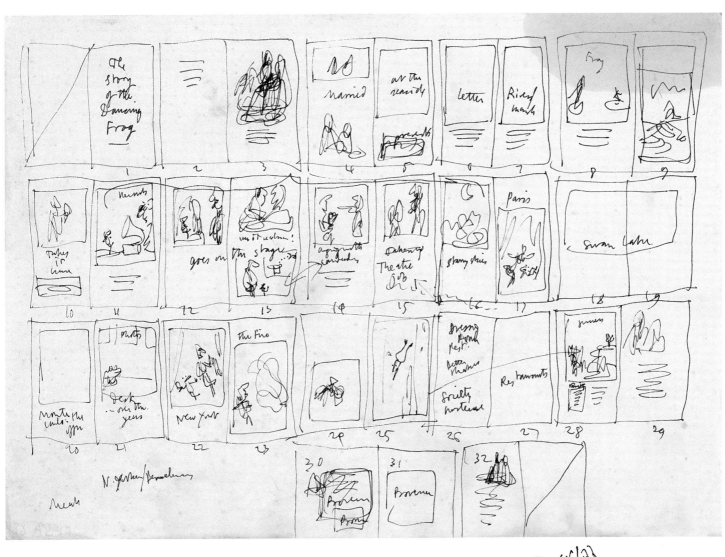

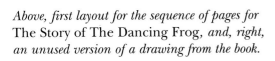

Above, first layout for the sequence of pages for
The Story of The Dancing Frog, *and,* right,
an unused version of a drawing from the book.

publish the book unless the person in that scene was white and wore more clothes; so that in the final version the part was given to Mistinguett with the frog jutting his lower lip as a kind of tiny Maurice Chevalier. In any case, I fully took the force of the objection. Most people looking at the book would probably not know who Josephine Baker was, even if I had named her; and the form of the book hardly allowed me to put in the message: "She is here because she is a heroine". Mysteriously, however, for reasons I am quite unable to account for, she did put in an appearance in the Spanish paperback; perhaps such a significant figure was not prepared to be overlooked altogether.

Above, the censored Josephine Baker and right, Mistinguett.

Facing page, life in retirement in Provence.

Two roughs and the final version for the grenier *in* Cockatoos.

The circumstances of one idea, one area of interest, encountering another was also what gave birth to *Cockatoos.* I have liked birds, to look at and to draw, ever since I was a child; and more recently I have found that if you need an extra note of colour, or an additional element to balance the composition of a picture, a small parrot, parakeet or cockatoo is a very useful standby; especially since, as the creature can fly, it can be introduced anywhere. So, as I had had a dancing frog in mind, I also had cockatoos; and I had searched unsuccessfully for some time for a way of involving a man with a troupe of birds. I found the answer about ten years ago when I was looking for a house to purchase in France. I was especially interested in one house, though in the end it was not the one I bought, because almost nothing in it had been changed since it was built a hundred years before. There was a conservatory, the traditional cellar, an ancient stove with its long metal chimney; and, as I climbed the steep stairs to the *grenier,* there in front of me was a row of suitcases arranged just as you see them in *Cockatoos.* All that was lacking was a cockatoo behind each.

He climbed a ladder
  and flashed his torch around the attic.
    They weren't there.

The story, now that I had found a home for it, became a counting book as well as a game of hide-and-seek. The situation here was not that of a group of characters acting and reacting in front of the necessary minimum of background; on the contrary, each picture had to be an accumulation of still life through which the reader browses in the search for our feathered friends. It's possible by the arrangement of elements in a picture to direct, at least to some extent, the eye of the beholder to move where you wish it to (the Old Masters had all this at their fingertips). Here the idea was to do without that and there had to be at least the appearance of a certain amount of clutter, because noting it on the way was intended as part of the entertainment. (It was naturally also part of my entertainment; the kitchen contains everything characteristically French that I could remember that might possibly be there.)

Left, a checklist of cockatoos and, right, roughs for the cover.

COCKATOOS

QUENTIN BLAKE

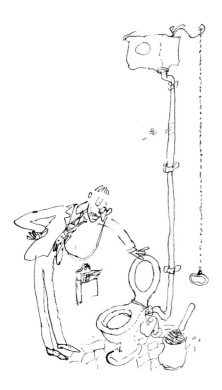
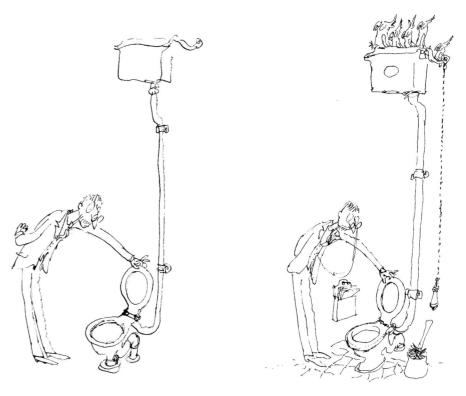

Three versions of the W.C.

It is evident that part of the practical force of the picture book for a small child is the ability to cross-check between words and pictures: we read "cat" and there it is. Later, when we feel more assured, there is the pleasure of noticing the disparities between the text and the pictures. The French have a useful word for this effect: *décalage* – the way two things don't fit together – like the shift of time between one country and another. It is an old and useful tool in the picture book maker's kit, and *Cockatoos* could not exist without it. The text is entirely from poor baffled Professor Dupont's point of view; the written story hasn't the first idea about the naughtiness that is going on in the pictures. As one friend put it to me: "When I read it to my son I am reading one story in the words and he is reading another story in the pictures."

But – a story about an out-of-date professor and a lot of birds amongst the furniture and fittings of a foreign country a hundred years ago – was this the stuff of a picture book for small children? Well, as it fortunately turned out, it was. Part of its attraction was undoubtedly the element of hide-and-seek; and part, I can't help suspecting, was that its readers, whether consciously or not, had noticed the similarity of the situation to that of a teacher rather set in his ways faced with a class of lively pupils.

magenta
+ little Venetian Red

Prof. Dupont:
his suit.

Establishing the colour for Professor Dupont's suit.

He went down into the cellar; but he couldn't see any cockatoos there, either.

I seem to remember, not so long ago, a reviewer observing that my picture books tend to be about a solitary, perhaps slightly eccentric, character attempting to cope, with whatever degree of success. That got me thinking about another aspect of picture books and allowed me to realise that, if my stories are concerned with idiosyncratic individuals, those of John Yeoman frequently involve some group collaboration; sometimes with the intended result (as in *Mouse Trouble* or *The Wild Washerwomen*) and sometimes not (as in *The Do-It-Yourself House That Jack Built*). Perhaps some of that spirit of collaboration leaked into *Cockatoos*; but, by contrast, the idiosyncratic individual observation is undoubtedly true of *Mrs Armitage on Wheels*. The structure of the story (like that of *Sixes and Sevens*) used the old folktale principle of accumulation – getting another person to hold on to the turnip, adding another ingredient to the nail soup – which is so well adapted to being shown visually. On this occasion the addition of extra items to Mrs Armitage's bicycle leads with ease to an enjoyable catastrophe, and that in its turn to the restarting of the sequence hinted at in the appearance of rollerskates. The idea, of course, is to leave the reader's imagination at work; and that it had that effect at least sometimes was very gratifyingly demonstrated by the number of children's drawings, continuing or repeating the story, that I have since received – more than for any other book.

It was one particularly lively continuation which came to me from a school in France that put the idea into my head of devoting another book to Mrs Armitage and her faithful dog Breakspear. If you are a young illustrator it is reassuring to embark on a series of books, and be able to look forward to future employment; but, much as I have enjoyed the company of Agaton Sax and Monster and above all the lovely Arabel and Mortimer, the older I get the less I want the commitment to repeating the same performance several times over. And although Mrs Armitage was insistent, it was in the interest of something new that I didn't pursue the rollerskate ideas so convincingly put forward by *les petits Français* but took my heroine to the seaside. It is, after all, one of my favourite places, and surfing, a sport genuinely of our time, qualified very well as one of the energetic physical activities which I like to draw without there being the slightest possibility of my engaging in them in real life.

Moreover, now that Mrs Armitage was firmly established in my affections as well as those of others, it gave me the opportunity both to renew her image (for her to be "*relooké*", as the French say) in *Mrs Armitage and the Big Wave* with something more funky by way of costume, as well as to give her a success instead of a disaster.

From Mrs Armitage on Wheels.

Cover illustration for Mrs Armitage
and the Big Wave.

Illustrations from the books about Arabel and Mortimer.

Above and next page, "captions" for the children's television programme Jackanory.
This picture shows the first appearance of Mortimer on the small screen.

The television camera followed the motorbike around this panoramic scene.

From Up With Birds!

Those two books exist essentially for the visual amusement they afford; but I think it must have been about this time that (perhaps because I was now free of my teaching commitments) I began to feel the need to get even more into the exploration of picture books. *Ten Frogs* for instance, which first appeared as *Dix Grenouilles,* is a counting book without any narrative structure; an attempt to change the scale of the page with big simple pictures which allowed me to draw with a brush and produce what were for me relatively naturalistic drawings. It is a surprisingly simple fact, but the amount of items – animals, people, objects – to be depicted in a book radically influences the ways in which it can be drawn. This was underlined for me by *Ten Frogs* and nicely

demonstrated in two books about birds by John Yeoman. The first, *Up with Birds!* about the time, not so long ago, before birds had discovered how to fly and encumbered the streets by walking everywhere, had a cast of dozens and dozens of them. To get in all the detail of gesture and expression and activity needed a pretty sharp nib. *The Heron and the Crane*, by contrast, is a retelling of a traditional folktale which has only two characters; they can't decide whether to get married or not, and with their indecisions and fits of temperament they are a trial to each other. It is natural to show them in close-up, so it was possible to draw them with a brush; and that led easily to the use of watercolour to show dramatic skies which reflect their moods.

5
Cinq rats

From Dix Grenouilles.

On the left, an illustration from The Heron and the Crane *with atmospheric use of watercolour. On this page, three attempts to find the best interpretation for the next picture in the book.*

Preliminary page layouts and, right, a full page rough for Clown.

As often with folktales and fables, the two birds behave like human beings. Unfortunately, it isn't easy to have new ideas for stories which refer, by a kind of metaphor, to real life; at least, it isn't easy for me. I just have to try to keep an open mind and stay on the alert. So, in respect of *Clown*, I am unable to explain why and how the idea surfaced when it did. All I can remember is that I was sitting on the shady side of the lawn in France one summer, trying to make something of the image of the Green Ship which I had woken up with one morning, when Clown also appeared. I think it was the way the little figure moved that appealed to me first – its mixture of being anatomical and also non-anatomical, so that it could go into the loose contortions that dismay the skinhead's dog. On the basis of one or two such incidents, and the initial premise of the toys being dumped into the dustbin, I began, for a short while, to write the story, until I realised that to explain in words the situation of rejection, and that some toys (like people) are invested with a greater sense of independent life than others etcetera, etcetera, was going to be too much for a picture book to sustain, and that what a miniature mime artist needs is a story without words. I found myself back in the beloved world of telling a story in pictures, and the tradition which extends to our own time with masters such as Sempé and Reiser, and of which Caran d'Ache is the great predecessor and Buster Keaton the patron saint. Though the possible economies of such a form are striking, it also brings its own special problems, so that if every emotional reaction and every step of the story has to be signalled by gesture, you just need more pictures, and if someone does speak, what you get in the speech balloon has to be not words but another picture. It's also important, both for the look and rhythm of the thing, to balance these small pictures with larger ones that show where and in what sort of place the events are happening. When the book was reviewed on French radio, one of the first things they recognised – no doubt because the reviewers were familiar with their own tradition of strip cartoon, the *bande dessinée* or BD – was that each double-page spread formed a sort of chapter on its own. In many respects this open-plan way of telling a story in pictures is different from the BD approach; there, the fact that everything in the narrative sequence is represented complete within a frame with its drawn background produces what is often quite a leisurely pace and a strange sense of reassurance even when the settings are

intergalactically bizarre, as they frequently are. It is nevertheless sometimes convenient to make use of characteristic BD effects: Clown falling through the tree, for instance, which divides itself into three consecutive moments, is an obvious one.

As I have explained, I did not set about *Clown* with the specific intention of creating a book without words; but, once it had appeared, its wordlessness proved to be interesting, sometimes in ways that I had not envisaged. One or two conversations suggested to me that there are parents who are dissatisfied that they do not have a text all set out ready for them (I acknowledge that the ritual of text-reading is important) and that they are going to have to make an effort of interpretation and discussion. Some such effort, however, is always called for, especially in a collaborative reading; and one of the incidental interests of a book like this is perhaps that it prevents you from assuming that you know a book because you have recited the words, in the same way that people assume they have grasped the Mona Lisa because their gaze has passed over its surface. Teachers, by contrast, were ready to seize on the book for this very reason. What is going on, and can we talk about it? It was good to see, in one school enterprise in Arles, large coloured photocopies displayed with dialogue in speech balloons added by the children. The interpretation of any story, of course, goes deeper than this, which leaves plenty of opportunity for speculation and discussion.

A final illustration for Clown *and, right, the rough for the return home in the evening.*

The final version of the return home. Clown reappears,
right, on a poster for a travelling exhibition in France.

Exposition à la Bibliothèque Elsa Triolet • Pantin
102 avenue Jean Lolive, 93500 Pantin, téléphone 49 15 45 04, métro: Eglise de Pantin
du 30 novembre 1995 au 17 janvier 1996

The British Council

Gallimard
Jeunesse

Ville de Pantin

Centre de promotion
du livre de jeunesse
Seine-Saint-Denis

Seine Saint-Denis
Conseil Général

There are many good children's books which deal with everyday life, the life of parents and children, in a straightforward descriptive way; and there are those which deal head-on with contemporary problems. It is absolutely proper and necessary that it should be so. Nevertheless, there are advantages, it seems to me, in stories which are like some kind of fable; which are not a direct transcription of everyday life. They can convey meaning in less direct ways, and to a wider audience; and they invite imagination

My memory is that I not so much dreamt as woke up with the image of the Green Ship in my head; and at that stage I made a rough note of it with no confidence that the idea would extend to the requirements of a picture book, let alone have any "fable" quality. When in due course I decided I must set to and try to work out a narrative I think it was help from an impeccable maritime source – Joseph Conrad and in particular *The Shadow Line* – that got me through and into the possibilities of the situation. One of these was the business of being able to merely hint at a lot of the story, such as the missing captain and the origin of the ship itself. In addition to that there was the technical fascination which came from the fact that the ship was unable to move but everything else could, so that you see the ship

from a variety of points of view – for instance the three pictures of the ship "moving" from left to right in the changing light of the day. It's something that, I hope, corresponds to the imagination that children use in play; Mrs Tredegar, steering the Green Ship through the storm, shares in this play; but for her it is serious. I have to confess that I do not know how much of the significance of this will be evident to children. I hope that they may at least view it as a piece of life happening before them to which they may bring varying degrees of comprehension.

   The story is also about time and memory, and this for me gave the final few pages of the book a special interest. When I wanted to show the ship growing out, growing back into trees, I could not help being reminded of the pleasure that I had as a child of comparing two similar pictures to note the changes and variations between them. I hope that pleasure will invite the reader to turn back the pages and so perform, in three-dimensional book terms, a little act of memory. At the same time those pages make use of that useful technique of tension between words and image, so that while the text is sadly telling us about the disappearance of the ship the illustration shows us that the trees themselves are bursting out with greenness and renewal.

Eventually it became so hot that
Mrs Tredegar decided that we must have
reached the Equator, and that we must
have the ceremony of Crossing the Line.
The Bosun was King Neptune, with a gold
cardboard crown and a hayfork for a
trident.

First-timers had to be shaved;
which seemed to include Alice as well
as me. There was a bucket of soapsuds
and a sort of wooden butterknife from
the kitchen, and we all got very wet.

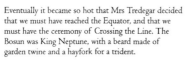

Eventually it became so hot that Mrs Tredegar decided
that we must have reached the Equator, and that we
must have the ceremony of Crossing the Line. The
Bosun was King Neptune, with a beard made of
garden twine and a hayfork for a trident.

First-timers had to be shaved; which seemed to include
Alice as well as me. There was a bucket of soapsuds
and a sort of wooden butterknife from the kitchen, and
we all got very wet.

The rough and the finished version of a spread from The Green Ship.

On this and the following two pages, unused versions of the storm from The Green Ship.

Though I think *The Green Ship* could not have had any other title, it took me a long while to name *Zagazoo*. At the same time I felt that I had been very lucky not only to have another idea (that is always a miracle) but to have one in many ways so different. It's obvious that this story depends entirely on visual metaphor; a world in which, if a child behaves like a little elephant, it is a little elephant. What I was anxious to achieve was to keep the book entirely within the conventions of such a world. In *The Green Ship* the surroundings comfortably cushion the narrative, while here the story takes place nowhere but on the page. It's a graphic world, where babies arrive by post and you are allowed to throw them in the air, and where you do not change your pullover, which just gently fades as you get older.

This book, once again, comes out of the adult tradition of humorous drawing; but it also nods to the conventions of artists such as Ionesco and Beckett; and because it does so, and goes into one or two transformations that might be unsettling to loving parents, I wondered if it might prove to be difficult of access. Fortunately, both adults and children seem able to relate happily to it, if not in quite the same way. Parents recognise the stages of development, and that has led one or two reviewers to regard it as not really for children; but the children themselves have not had a problem with it, at least as far as I have been able to find out. After all, the possibilities of being able to turn, at least in your imagination, into a variety of unexpected disruptive creatures, has its own fascination.

Facing page, a rough and the finished version of a spread from Zagazoo.

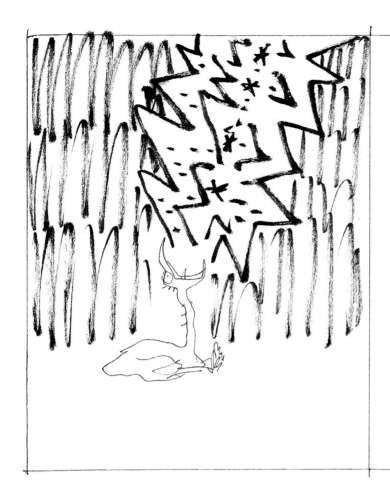

They were even worse at night.
"What shall we do?" said George. "How can we stand it?"

But then...

They were even worse at night.

"What shall we do?" said George.
"How can we stand it?"

But then...

The last picture book that I am able to write about was not intended to have the ambitions of *The Green Ship* or *Zagazoo*, although I think it did turn out to have characteristics of its own. *Fantastic Daisy Artichoke* was an attempt to return to the world of *Mr Magnolia* and you can see that it has the same sort of simple rhyming structure. Even so, it was more complicated to begin with; as I worked on it the book got simpler, and Daisy Artichoke got younger and more attractive: favourite young aunt, teacher, au pair. All that was left of the previous complications were the words: "We remember" – a prompt for conversations about people that you remember.

Unfortunately a book with this rhyming structure offers difficulties in translation which might limit its publication in any

Two unused illustrations from Fantastic Daisy Artichoke.

but English-speaking countries. (Except Holland; the Dutch seem able to translate anything from English into Dutch; they even translated *Cockatoos* from prose into Dutch rhyming couplets, out of sheer high spirits.) That led me to think what might happen in French, the only other language of which I have any knowledge, and I discovered that the problem I envisaged did not exist. Quite the reverse, in fact, since there are only a handful of rhymes for artichoke, whereas for *artichaut* there are hundreds; so that I found myself not only (with a little help) making up a parallel French version but also faxing my editor with further incidents which had a tendency to forget that they started in a children's picture book.

What was particularly interesting to me about the book was

The pond in which
she liked to soak

Her lovely ragged
patchwork cloak

that once again it was a question of large simple pictures; no expressions on the faces of mice had to be drawn, so that I could use a waterproof crayon – Karisma black – which gives the drawings a different scale and feel. You hold a clutch of them in your left hand and re-sharpen them every few minutes.

If I look back over the picture books of recent years – my own and the diversity of the works of others, both veterans and newcomers – I think I can see the prospects for the picture book open out and become more various; not merely in technique, but in the way that it has split open its nursery constraints and is now available for contemplation and discussion well beyond the nursery ages. If I am happy to have *Fantastic Daisy Artichoke* end this book it is not because it reflects any of the wider or deeper responses that a picture book can sometimes embrace (except perhaps affection). What I hope it has is those pleasures of being and doing, which make up a lot of life and which adults and children can share, celebrated in drawing; which is one of the specialities of that ever-interesting activity.

Biography

1932	Born in Sidcup, Kent, England.
1937-51	Attends local primary school and Chislehurst and Sidcup Grammar School.
1949	First drawings accepted for *Punch* magazine.
1951-3	National Service in the Royal Army Educational Corps.
1953-6	Reads English Literature at Downing College, Cambridge as a pupil of F.R. Leavis.
1956-7	Postgraduate certificate in Education at the Institute of Education of London University.
1958-9	Part-time student at Chelsea College of Art, under the guidance of Brian Robb.
1959-70	Illustrator and cover artist for *Punch* and *The Spectator*. Book jackets for Penguin Books.
1960	Publication of first illustrated children's book, *A Drink of Water* by John Yeoman.
1965	Part-time tutor in the Illustration Department of the Royal College of Art.
1968	Publication by Jonathan Cape of *Patrick*, the first book of which he is author and illustrator.
1972-6	Exhibitions at Mel Calman's Workshop Gallery: Invitation to the Dance; Runners and Riders; Creature Comforts; Water Music.
1978	First collaboration with Roald Dahl: *The Enormous Crocodile*.
1978-86	Head of the Illustration Department of the Royal College of Art.
1981	Elected RDI (Royal Designer for Industry).
1984	Retrospective of illustration work at The National Theatre.
1988	Senior Fellow and Visiting Professor of the Royal College of Art. Awarded OBE.
1990	Buys house in South West France.
1993	Chris Beetles Gallery: Exhibition of Roald Dahl illustrations.

1995	Exhibition: "Le Petit Théâtre de Quentin Blake" travels round France.
1996	Chris Beetles Gallery: The Art of Quentin Blake.
1999	Appointed first Children's Laureate. This appointment results in a number of projects, including: lectures and articles; the book *The Laureate's Party*, a choice of fifty favourite children's books; the preparation of an exhibition and an accompanying book for the National Gallery, *Tell Me A Picture*; and of an exhibition of contemporary children's book illustration for Bury St Edmunds Art Gallery.
	At the same time Quentin Blake writes and illustrates a children's picture book *Un Bateau Dans Le Ciel* in collaboration with 1500 French-speaking school children in South West France, London, Oslo and Luxembourg.
2000	Honorary Doctorate of The London Institute. Honorary Fellowship of Downing College, Cambridge. Chris Beetles Gallery: Retrospective exhibition for the launch of *Quentin Blake Words and Pictures*.

Meet Your Artist
QUENTIN BLAKE

Quentin Blake has had two of his books published in Picture Puffins so far – **PATRICK** and **ANGELO** – and did the drawings for **MY FRIEND MR LEAKEY**. He has also illustrated many other children's books, and teaches at the Royal College of Art. When we tried to find out more details about his life, he sent us the following story in pictures which he says is, 'well, almost all true…'

A brief autobiography from Puffin Post *in 1973.*

The photos on this page and page 188 are by Linda Kitson.

From The Good Book Guide.

Bibliography

The list shows first editions in whatever language; so that for instance the illustrations to *Lo Scrigno della Meraviglie* were commissioned by Mondadori, though the book was also published later in England under its original title *The Box of Delights.*

1960

Come Here Till I Tell You	Patrick Campbell	Hutchinson
A Drink of Water and Other Stories	John Yeoman	Faber & Faber

1961

Albert the Dragon	Rosemary Weir	Abelard-Schuman
The Boy's Country Book	John Moore	Collins
The Boy Who Sprouted Antlers	John Yeoman	Faber & Faber
Good Morning, Miss Dove	Frances Gray Patton	Penguin
The Wonderful Button	Evan Hunter	Abelard-Schuman

1962

Constantly in Pursuit	Patrick Campbell	Hutchinson
Listen and I'll Tell You	Edward Korel	Blackie
My Son-in-Law the Hippopotamus	"Ezo"	Abelard-Schuman
Punky, Mouse for a Day	John Moreton	Faber & Faber

1963

Brewing up in the Basement	Patrick Campbell	Hutchinson
How to Become a Scratch Golfer	Patrick Campbell	Blond
Tales of a Wicked Uncle	Rupert Croft-Cooke	Jonathan Cape

1964

Further Adventures of Albert the Dragon	Rosemary Weir	Abelard-Schuman
Gardeners' Question Time	Loads, Gemmell and Sowerbutts	BBC
The Gentle Knight	Richard Schickel	Abelard-Schuman
Lucy	Joan Tate	Heinemann Educational
The Next-doors	Joan Tate	Heinemann Educational
The Oxford Books of Stories for Juniors (3 volumes 1964-1966)	James Britton (ed.)	OUP
Riddles, Riddles Everywhere	Ennis Rees	Abelard-Schuman
Uncle	J.P. Martin	Jonathan Cape

1965

Agaton Sax and the Diamond Thieves	Nils-Olof Franzen	André Deutsch
Aphrodisiacs in your Garden	Charles Connell	Barker
Motoring and the Motorist	Bill Hartley, Roy McCarthy	BBC
The P-P-Penguin Patrick Campbell	Kaye Webb (ed)	Penguin
Pun Fun	Ennis Rees	Abelard-Schuman
Rough Husbandry	Patrick Campbell	Hutchinson
Uncle Cleans Up	J.P. Martin	Jonathan Cape

1966

Aristide	Robert Tibber	Hutchinson
Around the World in Eighty Days	Jules Verne	Chatto & Windus
Gardeners' Question Time	Loads, Gemmell and Sowerbutts	BBC
Home Economics	Beryl Ruth	Heinemann
Uncle and his Detective	J.P. Martin	Jonathan Cape

1967

Bits and Pieces	Joan Tate	Heinemann
Give a Dog a Good Name	M. & A. Bilbow	Hutchinson
Living with Technology	H.P. Rickman	Hodder & Stoughton
Luke's Garden	Joan Tate	Heinemann
Puzzles for Pleasure and Leisure	Thomas L. Hirsch	Abelard-Schuman
Tiny Tall Tales	Ennis Rees	Abelard-Schuman
Uncle and the Treacle Trouble	J.P. Martin	Jonathan Cape

1968

Albert and the Dragon and the Centaur	Rosemary Weir	Abelard-Schuman
The Energy Men	Miles Tomalin	Hodder & Stoughton
Patrick	Quentin Blake	Jonathan Cape
Put on Your Thinking Cap	Helen Jill Fletcher	Abelard-Schuman
Success with English; the Penguin Course	Geoffrey Broughton	Penguin
Thoughts and Aphorisms from the Fruits of Meditation of Kosma Prutkov		Royal College of Art

1969

Agaton Sax and the Scotland Yard Mystery	Nils-Olof Franzen	André Deutsch
Alphabet Soup	John Yeoman	Faber & Faber
A Band of Angels		Gordon Fraser
The Bear's Winter House	John Yeoman	Blackie
The First Elephant Comes to Ireland	Nathan Zimelman	Follett (USA)
Gillygaloos and Gollywhoppers	Ennis Rees	Abelard-Schuman
Jack and Nancy	Quentin Blake	Jonathan Cape
Mr Horrox and the Gratch	James Reeves	Abelard-Schuman
Uncle and Claudius the Camel	J.P. Martin	Jonathan Cape
Your Animal Poems		Gordon Fraser

1970

Agaton Sax and the Max Brothers	Nils-Olof Franzen	André Deutsch
Angelo	Quentin Blake	Jonathan Cape
The Bear's Water Picnic	John Yeoman	Blackie
The Birthday Party	D. Mackay	Longman
Doctors and Nurses	D. Mackay	Longman
The Good Tiger	Elizabeth Bowen	Jonathan Cape
Hogmanay and Tiffany	Gillian Edwards	Geoffrey Bles
Kibby's Big Feat	Thomas I. Corddry	Follett (USA)
"Quote and Unquote"	P. & J. Holton	Arcadia Press

Poster illustration for Book Power, *National Book Week, 1994.*

Designed for the Youth Libraries Group of the Library Association by Quentin Blake: 1982

1971

Agaton Sax and the Criminal Doubles	Nils-Olof Franzen	André Detusch
The Ages of Man: from Savage to Sewage	Marcus Cunliffe	American Heritage Press (USA)
The Birds	Aristophanes (Trans: Dudley Fitts)	Lion & Unicorn Press
My Friend Mr Leakey	J.B.S. Haldane	Penguin
Play School Play Ideas	Ruth Craft	BBC
Puzzles and Quizzles	Helen Jill Fletcher	Abelard-Schuman
Sixes and Sevens	John Yeoman	Blackie
The Witch's Cat	Harwood Thompson	Blackie

1972

Agaton Sax and the Colossus of Rhodes	Nils-Olof Franzen	André Deutsch
McBroom's Wonderful One-Acre Farm	Sid Fleischman	Chatto & Windus
Mouse Trouble	John Yeoman	Hamish Hamilton
Pigeon of Paris	Natalie Savage Carlson	Blackie
The Reader's Digest Treasury of American Humor		American Heritage Press (USA)

1973

Agaton Sax and the London Computer Plot	Nils-Olof Franzen	André Deutsch
Eating	Frances Knowles and Brian Thompson	Longman
Monster Books (12 titles)	Ellen Blance and Anne Cook	Longman
Snuff	Quentin Blake	Jonathan Cape
Uncle and the Battle for Badgertown	J.P. Martin	Jonathan Cape
Wizards are a Nuisance	Norman Hunter	BBC

1974

Agaton Sax and the League of Silent Exploders	Nils-Olof Franzen	André Deutsch
The Armada Lion Book of Young Verse	Julia Watson (ed.)	Armada
Beatrice and Vanessa	John Yeoman	Hamish Hamilton
Great Day for Up!	Dr Seuss	Beginner Books (USA)
Grimble and Grimble at Christmas	Clement Freud	Puffin
How Tom Beat Captain Najork and His Hired Sportsmen	Russell Hoban	Jonathan Cape
Mind Your Own Business	Michael Rosen	André Deutsch
The Puffin Joke Book	Bronnie Cunningham	Puffin
Tales of Arabel's Raven	Joan Aiken	Jonathan Cape/ BBC

1975

Agaton Sax and the Haunted House	Nils-Olof Franzen	André Deutsch
The Incredible Kidnapping	Willis Hall	Heinemann
Lester at the Seaside	Quentin Blake	Collins
Lester and the Unusual Pet	Quentin Blake	Collins
A Near Thing for Captain Najork	Russell Hoban	Jonathan Cape
One Hundred and One Black Cats	Stephen Mooser	Scholastic (USA)
The Puffin Book of Improbable Records	Quentin Blake and John Yeoman	Puffin

1976

Agaton Sax and the Big Rig	Nils-Olof Franzen	André Deutsch
The Bed Book	Sylvia Plath	Faber & Faber
Here Comes McBroom	Sid Fleischman	Chatto & Windus
Horseshoe Harry and the Whale	Adele de Leeuw	Parents' Magazine Press (USA)
The Boy Who Sprouted Antlers (re-illustrated)	John Yeoman	Collins Young Lions
The Hunting of the Snark	Lewis Carroll	The Folio Society
The Worried Ghost	Seymour Reit	Scholastic (USA)

1977

The Adventures of Lester	Quentin Blake	BBC
Cold Comfort Farm	Stella Gibbons	The Folio Society
Monster Books (12 titles)	Ellen Blance and Anne Cook	Longman
Nonstop Nonsense	Margaret Mahy	Dent
Of Quarks, Quasars and Other Quirks	Sara Bewton (ed.)	Crowell (USA)
Play School Play Ideas 2	Carol Ward	BBC
Willie the Squowse	Ted Allan	Jonathan Cape
Wouldn't You Like to Know	Michael Rosen	André Deutsch
The Young Performing Horse	John Yeoman	Hamish Hamilton

1978

Agaton Sax and Lispington's Grandfather Clock	Nils-Olof Franzen	André Deutsch
The Enormous Crocodile	Roald Dahl	Jonathan Cape
Funny Business	Bronnie Cunningham	Puffin
The Great Piratical Rumbustification and The Librarian and the Robbers	Margaret Mahy	Dent

1979

The Bakerloo Flea	Michael Rosen	Longman
Custard and Company	Ogden Nash	Kestrel
A Feast of True Fandangles	Patrick Campbell	W.H. Allen
The Wild Washerwomen	John Yeoman	Hamish Hamilton

1980

Ace Dragon Ltd	Russell Hoban	Jonathan Cape
Arabel and Mortimer (3 titles)	Joan Aiken	Jonathan Cape/ BBC
Black Mischief	Evelyn Waugh	The Folio Society
Mister Magnolia	Quentin Blake	Jonathan Cape
The True History of Sir Tom Thumb		Holp Shuppan (Japan)
The Twenty-Elephant Restaurant	Russell Hoban	Jonathan Cape
The Twits	Roald Dahl	Jonathan Cape
What Difference does it make Danny?	Helen Young	André Deutsch

1981

Cyril Bonhamy v Madam Big	Jonathan Gathorne-Hardy	Jonathan Cape
George's Marvellous Medicine	Roald Dahl	Jonathan Cape
McBroom and the Great Race	Sid Fleischman	Chatto & Windus
Les Trucs du Détective et de l'Agent Secret	Georges Berton	Gallimard (France)

Shakespeare's

The Deal Theatre Project

WALMER CASTLE · Kent · 0304 375192 · 3-18 AUGUST 1990

Cover illustration for The Hermit and the Bear.

Up with Skool!	Tony Lacey (ed.)	Puffin
You Can't Catch Me	Michael Rosen	André Deutsch

1982

The BFG	Roald Dahl	Jonathan Cape
Joseph and the Amazing Technicolor Dreamcoat	Tim Rice and Andrew Lloyd Webber	Pavilion
Roald Dahl's Revolting Rhymes	Roald Dahl	Jonathan Cape
Rumbelow's Dance	John Yeoman	Hamish Hamilton
Scoop	Evelyn Waugh	The Folio Society
Mortimer's Cross	Joan Aiken	Jonathan Cape/ BBC
(3 titles)		
Quentin Blake's Nursery Rhyme Book	Quentin Blake	Jonathan Cape
Quick, Let's Get Out of Here	Michael Rosen	André Deutsch
The Witches	Roald Dahl	Jonathan Cape

1984

Animal Farm	George Orwell	The Folio Society
Crash! The Waldo and Wanda Book of Practical Hints	John Yeoman	Magnet
Cyril Bonhamy and Operation Ping	Jonathan Gathorne-Hardy	Jonathan Cape
The Hermit and the Bear	John Yeoman	André Deutsch
How the Camel Got His Hump	Rudyard Kipling	Macmillan
The Story of the Dancing Frog	Quentin Blake	Jonathan Cape

1985

Don't Put Mustard in the Custard	Michael Rosen	André Deutsch
The Giraffe and the Pelly and Me	Roald Dahl	Jonathan Cape
A Lamp for the Lambchops	Jeff Brown	Methuen
Mortimer Says Nothing	Joan Aiken	Jonathan Cape

1986

Ask Dr Pete	Peter Rowan	Jonathan Cape
Frankie's Hat	Jan Mark	Viking Kestrel
The Marzipan Pig	Russell Hoban	Jonathan Cape
Scrapbooks		
(2 titles)	Michael Rosen	Walker

1987

The Campbell Companion	Patrick Campbell, Ulick O'Connor (ed.)	Pavilion
Cyril of the Apes	Jonathan Gathorne-hardy	Jonathan Cape
Mrs Armitage on Wheels	Quentin Blake	Jonathan Cape
Sarah la Pas Belle	Patricia MacLachlan	Gallimard (France)
Scrapbooks		
(2 titles)	Michael Rosen	Walker

1988

Matilda	Roald Dahl	Jonathan Cape
Our Village	John Yeoman	Walker

From Old Mother Hubbard's Dog.

The Roald Dahl Guide to Railway Safety, *1991,
later inspired* Zap! The Quentin Blake Guide to
Electrical Safety, *1998.*

Electricity becomes _dangerous_ when there is a chance that it can escape.

So, to begin with, don't let little kids play around with or near electrical appliances.

And remember DON'T poke about in the electric toaster with a knife.

and DON'T poke anything into an electric socket.

1989

Quentin Blake's ABC	Quentin Blake	Jonathan Cape
Old Mother Hubbard's Dog	John Yeoman	Walker
Monsters	Russell Hoban	Gollancz
Rhyme Stew	Roald Dahl	Jonathan Cape

1990

Il Populo di Mezzanotte	John Masefield	Mondadori (Italy)
Esio Trot	Roald Dahl	Jonathan Cape
Alphabeasts	Dick King-Smith	Gollancz
Un Pirate dans la Ville	Jacqueline Balcells	Bayard (France)
All Join In	Quentin Blake	Jonathan Cape
La Casa Sull'Albero	Bianca Pitzorno	Mondadori (Italy)

From Le Terrible Trimestre de Gus.

1991

The World's Laziest Duck (Reissue of *The Puffin Book of Improbable Records*)	John Yeoman	Macmillan
The Vicar of Nibbleswick	Roald Dahl	Random Century
Algernon	Hilaire Belloc	Jonathan Cape
Voyages to the Sun and the Moon	Cyrano de Bergerac	The Folio Society
The Dahl Diary	Roald Dahl	Penguin
Ascolta il mio Cuore	Bianca Pitzorno	Mondadori (Italy)
Roald Dahl's Guide to Railway Safety	Roald Dahl	British Railways Board
Lo Scrigno delle Meraviglie	John Masefield	Mondadori (Italy)

1992

Cockatoos	Quentin Blake	Jonathan Cape
Mortimer and Arabel	Joan Aiken	BBC
Le Terrible Trimestre de Gus	Gene Kemp	Gallimard (France)
The Giraffe and the Pelly and Me (new ed.)	Roald Dahl	Jonathan Cape

1993

Featherbrains	John Yeoman	Hamish Hamilton
Simpkin	Quentin Blake	Jonathan Cape
My Year	Roald Dahl	Jonathan Cape
The Singing Tortoise	John Yeoman	Gollancz
The Family Album	John Yeoman	Hamish Hamilton
Cautionary Verses	Hilaire Belloc	Jonathan Cape
Barka	Jan Werich	Le Seuil (France)
La Zia ha Adottato un Lincantropo	Saki	Salani (Italy)
Polissena del Porcello	Bianca Pitzorno	Mondadori (Italy)
Pourquoi tu ne Manges pas Amélie Ramolla?	Aline Guichard	Bayard (France)

1994

Danny the Champion of the World	Roald Dahl	Jonathan Cape
The Winter Sleepwalker	Joan Aiken	Jonathan Cape
The Roald Dahl Quizbook 1	Richard Mather and Sylvia Bond (ed)	Puffin
The Do-It-Yourself House that Jack Built	John Yeoman	Hamish Hamilton
Roald Dahl's Revolting Recipes	Felicity Dahl and Josie Fison	Jonathan Cape
The Quentin Blake Book of Nonsense Verse	Quentin Blake (ed.)	Viking
Quentin Blake Agenda	Quentin Blake and John Yeoman	Fontein (Holland)

1995

Charlie and the Chocolate Factory	Roald Dahl	Viking
Charlie and the Great Glass Elevator	Roald Dahl	Viking
James and the Giant Peach	Roald Dahl	Viking
Mr Nodd's Ark	John Yeoman	Hamish Hamilton
Clown	Quentin Blake	Jonathan Cape
A Christmas Carol	Charles Dickens	Pavilion
Elephants Have Right of Way	Sylvia Sherry	Jonathan Cape
Meeting Midnight	Carol Ann Duffy	Prospero Poets
A Handful of Gold	Joan Aiken	Jonathan Cape
Diana, Cupido e il Commendatore	Bianca Pitzorno	Mondadori (Italy)
Breakfast with Dolly	John Hedgecoe	Collins & Brown
The Magic Finger	Roald Dahl	Viking
Don Quixote de la Mancha	Miguel de Cervantes	The Folio Society
La Vie de la Page	Quentin Blake	Gallimard (France)

1996

Fantastic Mr Fox	Roald Dahl	Viking
The Seven Voyages of Sinbad the Sailor	retold by John Yeoman	Pavilion
The Quentin Blake Book of Nonsense Stories	Quentin Blake (ed.)	Viking
The Roald Dahl Quizbook 2	Richard Mather and Sylvia Bond	Puffin
Re Mida ha le Orecchi d'Asino	Bianca Pitzorno	Mondadori (Italy)

1997

Mrs Armitage and the Big Wave	Quentin Blake	Jonathan Cape
The Princes' Gifts	John Yeoman	Pavilion
Dix Grenouilles	Quentin Blake	Gallimard (France)

1998

The Green Ship	Quentin Blake	Jonathan Cape
Up With Birds!	John Yeoman	Hamish Hamilton
Zagazoo	Quentin Blake	Jonathan Cape
The Twelve Days of Christmas	John Julius Norwich	Doubleday
Sarah la Pas Belle se Marie	Patricia McLachlan	Gallimard (France)
Zap! The Quentin Blake Guide to Electrical Safety		Eastern Electricity

1999

Drawing for the Artistically Undiscovered	John Cassidy	Klutz (USA)
Fantastic Daisy Artichoke	Quentin Blake	Jonathan Cape
The Heron and the Crane	John Yeoman	Hamish Hamilton
Trouble on Thunder Mountain	Russell Hoban	Faber & Faber
Woman with a Book. Twenty Watercolour drawings by Quentin Blake with an introduction by Russell Hoban		Camberwell Press

From The Art Quarterly, 2000

Overleaf, "The Poor Children and The Strange Bird", May 2000.

2000

The Laureate's Party	Quentin Blake	Random House
Wizzil	William Steig	Farrar Straus Giroux (USA)
Your Child's Learning Journey: the parents' guide to the National Curriculum		DfEE
Un Bateau dans Le Ciel	Quentin Blake	Rue du Monde
Quentin Blake Words and Pictures	Quentin Blake	Jonathan Cape

Mr Magnolia was the winner of the Kate Greenaway Medal and the Children's Book Award of the Federation of Children's Book Groups in 1980; *All Join In* of the Kurt Maschler Award in 1990; and *Clown* of the Ragazzi Prize at the Bologna Children's Book Fair in 1996.